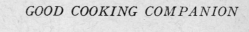

GOOD COOKING COMPANION

Mary Gallati's

GOOD COOKING COMPANION

ABBEY LIBRARY

146 – 152 Holloway Road, London N. 7

WITH AFFECTIONATE APPRECIATION TO

MARIO (MY FATHER) OF THE CAPRICE

HIS PATRONS

HIS STAFF

GRATEFUL ACKNOWLEDGMENT AND THANKS TO

CHEF GEORGE ALLOUIS

MAJ. RAFAEL CALZADA

typography and decorations by

RAYMOND E. MEYLAN, M.S.I.A.

Unless otherwise stated or
understood, recipes are suitable
for a family quantity of
approximately four

CONTENTS

INDEX

INDEX

INDEX

INDEX

FOREWORD

I was fortunate to receive enthusiastic approval and appreciation of the "Hostess Dinner Book", but there were resultant comments, such as

"What about the bachelor or the bachelor-girl who fends for him/herself?"
"What about the student in the kitchen?"
"Or the new bride who has to feed the brute?"
"How about the housewife who has to cook every day and dish up something different, especially in the way of left-overs?"

Well, as one thing leads to another, so a challenge arose to try and write a general cookery guide combining handiness with common sense ; that is to say, not only the selection, purchase, preparation and presentation of food in a variety of interesting ways, but, also, the utilization of remnants into attractive edible recipes instead of the frequent shameful waste of discarding them or cooking them indifferently.

Thus, in pursuit of an idea to answer the challenge, this book emerged—meant to be gastronomically practical and yet with appetizing recipes suitable for daily use or for presentation to your best guest.

It contains economy, but economy, of course, in its true culinary sense—not insufficient use of food but making the best of what you have or can have.

The book has classified divisions to simplify cooking recipes for each particular food item purchased.

I have tried to follow through every stage of each food product, in fact, to depict its progress from the time of purchase and selection, its various cooking recipes, on to the final left-overs.

I do hope it succeeds in being equally valuable to the bride, the student, the epicure and the housewife ; in fact, proves to be a satisfactory cookery companion in your very own kitchen.

Bon appétit !

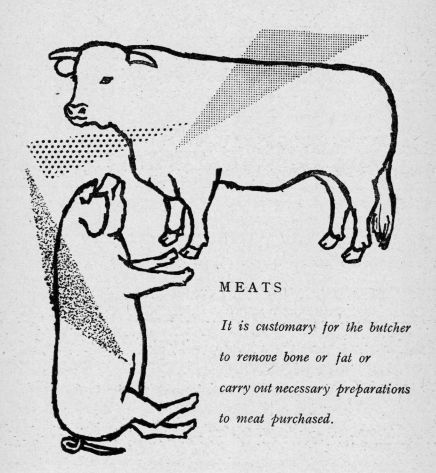

MEATS

*It is customary for the butcher
to remove bone or fat or
carry out necessary preparations
to meat purchased.*

LAMB

In season all the year round but, generally, best in the spring. (Grass-lamb from Easter to Michaelmas and house-lamb from Christmas to Lady-Day.)
Flesh of lamb is a pale rose colour and has firm pearly white fat; should feel firm to the touch for, if flabby, will be flavourless.

MUTTON

In season all the year round but best in spring, autumn and winter.
Good mutton is deeper pink, almost red, has small bones and is plump without being over fat; flesh should be firm and fat thick and waxy in texture.
Whether mutton is preferred to that of the ewe and is recognized by the lump of fat on the inside of the thigh.

Mutton, of course, takes much longer to cook than lamb.

LAMB AND MUTTON

BEST END

Nearest loin and is neatly divided into chops.

BASIC WAYS OF COOKING

LAMB. A good roast; if cut into chops or cutlets—fry, grill.
MUTTON. Young—grill, roast. Old—stew.

DOUBLE LAMB CUTLET

1 *double lamb cutlet (per portion). Sprig of watercress.*

Grill the cutlet for 15 minutes; when ready, garnish with watercress.

You may use pieces of best end of mutton for: Irish Stew (see Shoulder, page 11); Lancashire Hot Pot (see Scrag End of Neck, page 8).

BREAST

Reasonable joint, fatty, with thin stripes of meat.

BASIC WAYS OF COOKING

Braise, stew, bone and roll and roast.

EPIGRAMS

Epigrams (lamb or mutton chest or breast). Court-bouillon, without vinegar. Egg. Bread-crumbs.

Cook epigrams in court-bouillon for $1\frac{1}{2}$ hours; when ready, remove and bone it, and allow to cool. Cut into large "finger" pieces, egg and bread-crumb, and fry or grill them. Serve immediately with Béarnaise Sauce.

An economical dish I would suggest for your home cuisine, so often ignored yet very nice indeed, is the following—

3

BREAST OF YOUNG LAMB PERSILLÉ

Have the breast of very young lamb cut into 3-inch pieces (by your butcher), season, and roast in the normal manner; when ready, mix well together 2 parts bread-crumbs, 1 part grated cheese and pinch of parsley, and spread this mixture over the pieces of lamb with a pat of butter on top; grill until golden brown and serve at once.

STUFFED ROAST BREAST OF LAMB OR MUTTON

1 breast of lamb or mutton. Veal stuffing (see Stuffings, page 182). Knob of dripping.

Remove bones from the breast, trim surplus fat, and spread stuffing on the meat; roll up tightly and tie with fine string. Place in a roasting-tray with sprinkling of flour and dripping. Roast.

LEG

SHANK END—more juicy and tender than fillet end.
FILLET END—tends to be a little bit drier but more edible meat on the fillet end than the shank end.
(Haunch is the leg with part of loin attached.)

BASIC WAYS OF COOKING

Boil, roast.

ROAST LEG OF LAMB

1 leg (shoulder or saddle of lamb also suitable). Seasoning of salt and pepper.

Season the lamb, place in a tray with fat and roast in a fast oven for 10 minutes. Reduce the heat and roast until cooked, basting from time to time. (Roasting time—20 minutes to each pound, 20 minutes over.) When ready, keep hot and allow to settle 15 minutes before carving.

For the Gravy—pour the fat from the tray slowly, retaining the sediment and meat juice. Place the tray on the fire, reduce to a glaze, add just enough stock (vegetable water, if none) required, cook for 5 minutes; correct seasoning.
Serve separately.
Carve the meat at the very last moment and serve on very hot plates. Serve with mint sauce or mint jelly (outside purchase) or redcurrant jelly.

Leg of lamb carries less fat than mutton; therefore, yields more meat suitable for Curry, Minced Lamb, Moussaka. (For recipes see Remnants, page 13).

ROAST LEG OF MUTTON

(Shoulder or Saddle of Mutton also suitable)
Same as for Leg of Lamb but cooking takes longer.
Serve with onion sauce or redcurrant jelly.

The following is a wonderful winter dish:

BOILED LEG OF MUTTON

(Shoulder or Saddle of Mutton also suitable)
1 *leg*.
Boil (20 minutes to the lb., 15 minutes over).
Serve with Caper Sauce.

LOIN (RIBS)

SADDLE—double loin undivided.

DIVIDED—best end and chump end.

LOIN CHOPS—small and neat, with long tails of bone and fat.

CHUMP CHOPS—cut from chump end of loin and are larger with more meat and less bone but not quite as tender as loin chops; may be cut thick or thin.

5

LOIN. An excellent roast ; if cut into chops—fry, grill.

CUTLETS. Fry, grill. (Cutlets appetizing beaten with wooden spoon first, then fried in a coat of egg and breadcrumbs.)

SADDLE OF LAMB AU ROMARIN

1 *saddle of lamb (or mutton).* $\frac{1}{4}$ *pint stock.* 12 *potatoes. Sprig of rosemary. Seasoning of salt and pepper.*

Skin the saddle, tie at each end with string, season. Place on a bed of peeled potatoes, preferably all the same size, sprinkle with a little rosemary. Place in the oven and roast for 45 to 50 minutes (for mutton—1 to $1\frac{1}{4}$ hours). Remove saddle and potatoes. Carefully drain off the fat so as to leave the sediment ; re-heat on the fire until the sediment is beginning to brown in the bottom of the pan ; drain off any fat which may be left in the pan ; add stock and simmer for 10 minutes. Season. Strain.

The saddle may be re-formed on the bone, if desired, and surrounded by the roast potatoes on the serving-dish.

Serve separately—mint sauce or redcurrant jelly, and gravy.

With lamb or mutton chump chops or cutlets which are not too tender—

MUTTON CHOPS CHAMPVALLON

4 *mutton chops.* 2 *large onions, peeled and shredded.* $1\frac{1}{2}$ *lb. potatoes, peeled and sliced. Seasoning of salt and pepper.* 1 *pint stock or water. Chopped parsley.*

Mix potatoes and onions together, season. Shallow-fry the chops until brown. Place a layer of potatoes in a fireproof dish or casserole dish ; add the chops, cover with remainder of potatoes ; finish the final layer by forming the potatoes into a pattern ; add stock or water. Place in the oven and cook for 1½ to 2 hours. Remove, tilt and remove all the surplus fat. Sprinkle with chopped parsley. Serve very hot.

KHEBAB À LA GRECQUE

Loin of lamb. 8 mushrooms. 8 leaves of mint. Seasoning of chopped onion, parsley, salt and pepper. ¼ teaspoon oil.

Bone loin of lamb, remove nerves and most of the fat, and cut into cubes. Season. Put eight of the cubes on a skewer with a mushroom and a leaf of mint between each one and grill.
Serve with rice prepared as follows : —

½ onion, chopped. 2 chipolata sausages, cut in pieces. 2½ cups stock. 1 oz. butter. 1 cup Carolina rice. 1 pimento, diced. 1 tomato, diced. Seasoning of salt and pepper.

Fry onion and sausages in butter, and when brown add rice, pimento, tomato and stock ; season to taste, cover and cook in oven till dry ; then add butter and mix well.
Arrange in a hot dish, put the Khebab on top, add a little Madeira sauce and a little browned butter.
For Khebab à l'Orientale, cook rice same as for La Grecque, but in addition a pinch of saffron and a few chopped mint leaves.

This is a delightful picnic dish as Shish Khebab skewers can be broiled over a small wood fire :

SHISH KHEBAB

One of each of the following skewered alternately on long skewers : —

Loin of lamb, cut in 1½-inch cubes. Squares of onion. Whole mushrooms. Quarters of fresh tomatoes. Bay-leaves. Slices of fresh red or green peppers. (If desired, small pieces of bacon may be added.)

Broil for 15 to 20 minutes, turning skewers from time to time. When ready, serve each portion on a bed of rice pilaff.

You may use pieces of loin for: Curry (see Remnants, page 13), Irish Stew (see Shoulder, page 11), Lancashire Hot Pot (see Scrag End of Neck, page 8), Meat Pie (see Remnants, page 13), Minced Lamb (see Remnants, page 14), Moussaka à l'Algérienne (see Remnants, page 14).

SCRAG END OF NECK

Nearest head and, since meaty part of the top of shoulder is cut away from this part of neck, has a certain quantity of meatless bone. (Weight 1 to 2 lb.)

BASIC WAYS OF COOKING

Stew, also use for pies, soups, or stocks. (Cutlets contain a quantity of gristle, so they make a rich gravy and excellent Brown Stew.)

LANCASHIRE HOT POT

This recipe to ward off winter cold or fog comes from good old Lancashire and is a great favourite. A controversial dish, for "we beg to differ" as to its preparation since goodness-knows-when. Some prefer to treat it like a stew and simply boil the ingredients but the following is the recipe considered to extract the most flavour, and if anyone has a better recipe I should like to know it !

2 lb. scrag end of mutton or lamb (or loin, best end of mutton, shoulder); trim well all surplus fat, cut into large pieces. 4 tomatoes, blanched, peeled, and chopped into large dice. 2 onions,

peeled and shredded. 1 leek, washed well and cut into small dice. 2 carrots, washed, scraped and cut into fine rings. 4 cooking oysters (inexpensive good ones may be obtained), or 8 mussels, i.e., the "poor man's oysters".
1 pint water. 2 lb. potatoes, peeled and cut into fine slices. Seasoning of salt and pepper. Sprinkling of bread-crumbs.

Season and shallow-fry the pieces of lamb until brown, place in a casserole or saucepan. Shallow-fry onions, leek and carrots, for 2 minutes. Place on top of the meat, season well, add layers of tomatoes. Season potatoes and place on top in layers; add water, cover, bring to the boil. Then cook in the oven for 1 to 1½ hours. On removal, tilt to one side and skim carefully all fat; care should be taken that fat is drained off well. Add oysters or mussels, sprinkle with bread-crumbs, brown under the grill.
Serve very hot.

HARICOT LAMB OR MUTTON

2 lb. scrag end, trimmed and cut into small pieces. 2 onions, peeled and sliced. 2 turnips, peeled and sliced. 1 oz. flour. 1 oz. fat. 4 oz. haricot beans, washed and soaked overnight (cooked separately). 1½ lb. peas, shelled. 2 carrots, scraped and sliced. 1 pint stock or water. Bay-leaf. Seasoning of salt and pepper.

Put dripping in a pan; flour the meat pieces and fry quickly; remove meat. Add flour and stir until evenly browned; add stock and stir continually until boiling. Then add vegetables with the meat pieces, bay-leaf and seasoning. Let simmer for 2 hours on the stove or place in a casserole and cook in the oven. Add beans 15 minutes before serving.

With some neck, bones or ribs of mutton, make:

SCOTCH BROTH

Mutton, some neck or ribs. Diced carrots, leeks, onions, turnips, celery. Chopped parsley. 2 handfuls barley. Seasoning of salt and pepper.

Remove most of the fat from the neck or ribs, place them in cold water, bring to the boil, skim well, season. Add barley, carrots, leeks, onions, turnips, celery; season, and simmer slowly for 2½ hours. Correct seasoning. When ready, skim and remove meat. Cut meat into small dice. Before serving, add meat and chopped parsley.

You may use scrag end for: Irish Stew (see Shoulder, page 11), Curry (see Remnants, page 13), Meat Pie (see Remnants, page 13), Minced Lamb (see Remnants, page 14), Navarin (see Shoulder, page 11).

SHOULDER

Delicate, tender meat, not economical because rather fatty and including large blade-bone. (Weight 3 to 5 lb.)

BASIC WAYS OF COOKING

SHOULDER OF LAMB.	Braise, stew, bone and roll and stuff and roast. (After stuffing, sew up meat with string.) Actually, perfect for a roast, served with mint sauce, or redcurrant jelly, or mint jelly (outside purchase).
SHOULDER OF MUTTON.	Stew, boil (serve with caper sauce). Roast (serve with onion sauce).

SHOULDER OF LAMB BOULANGÈRE

1 shoulder of lamb. 2 lb. potatoes, peeled and finely sliced. 1 large onion, peeled and finely sliced. Seasoning of salt and pepper. 2 tablespoons water.

Place lamb in a tray and roast in the oven for 30 minutes. Remove carefully, strain off the fat and make the gravy. Season potatoes and onion, place them in roasting-tray, add water and fat from the lamb. Cook in the oven for 20 minutes. Place shoulder on top of potatoes and finish cooking together.

Various cuts of lamb or mutton may be used for the following two stews, i.e. shoulder or scrag:

NAVARIN

2 lb. shoulder or scrag of mutton or lamb (cut the shoulder-bone meat into dice; in the case of the scrag, split the scrag and cut into large sections, leaving the bones). 2 carrots, scraped and diced. 12 small onions, peeled. 2 turnips, peeled and diced. 1 lb. potatoes, peeled. 1 clove of garlic, finely chopped. 1 dessertspoon flour. 1 tablespoon tomato purée. 1 quart stock or water. Seasoning of salt and pepper. Chopped parsley.

Shallow-fry in a pan meat pieces in a little hot fat until browned ; dust with the flour and cook for 2 or 3 minutes. Add tomato purée ; mix well ; add stock and chopped garlic. Season. Bring to the boil, then simmer slowly. Meanwhile, shallow-fry together onions, carrots, turnips. Then add to the stew in the last hour of cooking so that these vegetables and stew are ready at the same time. Add the potatoes during the last half hour. Skim well to remove all fat. Sprinkle with chopped parsley.

IRISH STEW

2 lb. shoulder or scrag of lamb or mutton, or best end of mutton, cut into very large pieces. 4 large onions, peeled and sliced. 1 leek. 1 celery head. 2 lb. potatoes, peeled and finely sliced. ½ cup chopped parsley (coarsely chopped). Seasoning of salt and pepper.

Bring meat to the boil in plain water; boil for 5 minutes; then place in the sink under the cold tap and allow the water to rush through the meat; wash well. Replace in fresh water, add onions, leek and celery head; season, bring to the boil, add ½ lb. finely sliced potatoes. Simmer until nearly cooked, add remainder of potatoes; cover, simmer till cooked, skim well, correct seasoning. Just before serving, add parsley. (If desired, button onion may be added at the same time as the potatoes.)
Serve with dumplings, if desired.

You may use pieces of shoulder also for Lancashire Hot Pot (see Scrag End of Neck, page 8).

LAMB BARBECUE

In countries where there are "wide open spaces" they hold barbecues or outdoor parties with meat, such as grilled or fried steaks and chops, or roasts, cooked in the open air too. But, if it is a lovely day (especially at Eastertime so that you may choose spring lamb) and you live at the seaside, in the country, have a garden or a beach, and want an outdoor party, there is no reason why you should not hold a barbecue; apart from the fun involved, with the following recipe you may feed up to fifty people comfortably, merrily, and economically : —

1—30-lb. lamb. Seasoning of garlic and salt (or mixture of salt, pepper and mustard). Sprigs of parsley. Crate of lettuce. 1 bushel of potatoes.

Skin, wash and trim the lamb. Cut off head and feet (or have this done by your butcher). Crush garlic into salt and rub all over the meat, or rub alternative seasoning mixture into meat. When dressed, let it dry out. Split the lamb and tie it on to spit with wire. Turn and baste the meat regularly, letting anyone or everyone help to do this ! Joints will break open when cooked. Garnish with sprigs of parsley.

Serve each portion with jacket potatoes, lettuce salad, and hunks of fresh bread or rolls.

Have ready for self-service : Wine glasses and carafes of red wine or vin rosé.

SHEEP'S HEAD

Split and remove the brain, soak in cold water for 2 to 3 hours, wash well. Place in cold water, bring to the boil, skim well, add carrots, leeks, onions, sticks of celery, and seasoning of salt and pepper. Cook for 4 hours.

Lightly poach the brain in salted water.

Slice the tongue and cheek.

Serve in soup plates with the vegetables and a portion of the brain.

REMNANTS

Any lamb or mutton remnants may be used for :—

CURRY (see Rice, page 184)

MEAT PIE

Slices of cooked meat (any cooked meat is suitable). 2 large potatoes, peeled and sliced. ½ lb. tomatoes, peeled and sliced. Seasoning of salt and pepper. 1 cup stock. 1 onion, peeled and chopped. ½ lb. mushrooms, peeled and sliced. Browned bread-crumbs. Knob of butter.

Place in a greased pie-dish alternate layers of meat, potatoes, tomatoes, onions, mushrooms, and seasoning ; finish with a layer of potatoes. Add stock. Sprinkle with bread-crumbs and top

13

with butter. Cover with grease-proof paper and
bake for ¾ hour.

MINCED LAMB

*2 lb. minced lamb (uncooked or cooked). 1 cup
brown sauce. 1 measure of sherry. 1 onion,
peeled and finely chopped. Seasoning of salt
and pepper.*

If uncooked—fry and toss onion in butter until
golden brown, add minced lamb, season, stir well
for 10 minutes. Then place in greased casserole
dish with brown sauce and sherry and bake for
¾ hour. If cooked—place minced lamb in greased
casserole dish with brown sauce and sherry and
bake for 20 minutes.

MOUSSAKA À L'ALGÉRIENNE

*1 lb. minced lamb. 2 segments of garlic. 4 egg-
plants. 1 lb. tomatoes. 1 bouquet garni. 1 dessertspoon flour. ¼ pint brown stock. 1 large onion,
finely chopped. Seasoning of salt and pepper.*

Place a little fat in a saucepan, put in the chopped
onion and lightly fry. Add the meat, chopped
garlic, and cook for 10 minutes. Add the flour
and cook for 5 minutes. Add the stock and half
the tomatoes skinned and chopped. Season. Add
bouquet garni. Cook slowly for 1 hour.
Meanwhile, slice the eggplants lengthwise and
fry in oil ; arrange on an earthenware or fire-proof
dish, end to end, so that they hang over the side
of the dish. Place in the meat. Place the remainder of the tomatoes, skinned and sliced, on
the top. Bring up the ends of the eggplants to
completely cover the meat and tomatoes. (If
desired, sprinkle with grated cheese.) Cook in
the oven for 30 minutes.

There are two methods of service:—
1. Serve from the dish.
2. Turn on a flat dish and, if care has been taken with the lining of eggplants, a very beautiful effect is obtained.

With the left-overs of roasted lamb:

LAMB ORLOFF

Roasted lamb pieces, boned and cut into thin slices. 4 oz. cooked and minced mushrooms, well mixed together.

Arrange slices of meat in a greased pie-dish with mushroom mixture in between each slice. Cover with Mornay sauce and bake in a hot oven for 10 minutes.

With the left-overs of boiled or braised mutton:

CABBAGE DOLMAS

1 dozen medium-zised cabbage leaves, plunged in boiling water. Left-over boiled or braised mutton (boiled or braised beef also suitable). 3 table-spoons finely chopped onions, 3 tablespoons stale bread-crumbs, 3 tablespoons cooked rice. Seasoning of salt, chopped parsley and paprika. Slices of fat bacon.

Make a hash of left-over meat, onions, bread-crumbs, rice and seasoning; shape into "tangerine" sized balls. Roll up securely each hash ball into a cabbage leaf and cover each with bacon. Put all in a greased dish, cover with grease-proof paper and bake in a moderate oven for 1 hour. Serve with slices of lemon.

BEEF

In season all the year round.
Beef should be rich red and fine grained, and should be marbled or have an outer edge of creamy white fat or otherwise it tends to be dry.
Yellow fat indicates inferior meat.

AITCHBONE (EDGE-BONE)

Bone large in proportion to meat and, for this reason, sold at a cheaper rate than best joints.

BASIC WAYS OF COOKING

Braise, stew, boil. Excellent joint to boil.

SAUTÉ BEEF BOURGUIGNONNE

2 lb. suitable stewing meat, cut into 1-inch cubes. 24 small onions, peeled. ½ lb. mushrooms, washed and quartered. 2 oz. lean slices of bacon, cut into small cubes. 2 pints stock. 4 cloves of garlic, peeled and chopped. 1 tablespoon tomato purée. 1 dessert-spoon flour. Seasoning of salt and pepper. ¼ bottle Burgundy. 1 measure of brandy.

Shallow-fry the meat in a saucepan in a little fat until brown, add flour. Cook for 5 minutes. Add brandy, then burgundy wine. Stir in stock, tomato purée and garlic. Season. Cover and cook slowly for 1½ hours. Meanwhile, shallow-fry the bacon pieces with the onions and mushrooms. Add to the meat, cook for a further ¾ hour. Remove, skim well, correct seasoning, and serve immediately.

BRISKET

Excellent joint as fatty and not dry.

BASIC WAYS OF COOKING

Salt and boil, stew, braise. Also served as pressed beef, and used for meat pies or puddings, soups or stocks. When cooked fresh (unsalted), an excellent stock for soup may be extracted from it, yet the meat will serve as well for dinner : —

BEEF BROTH

Brisket (weight 1½ lb.). 2 quarts water. 3 small onions, peeled and sliced. 3 carrots, scraped and sliced. 2 parsnips, peeled and sliced. Leeks, peeled and sliced. Seasoning of salt, pepper and mixed herbs.

Bring meat to boil in water, skim; then lower the heat, cover, and let simmer for 4 or 5 hours. Add prepared vegetables during last hour of cooking. Skim again before serving with vegetables.

With the:

BOILED BRISKET OF BEEF

Serve the meat hot or cold, garnish with chopped parsley, accompany with Salsa Verde and a green seasonal salad.

FLANK

Fatty and cheaper than many cuts. Includes the "skirt"—good lean and cheap cut. Economical for the large family.

BASIC WAYS OF COOKING

Salt and boil, stew, pot-roast; also good served cold as pressed beef, and used for meat pies or puddings, soups or stocks.

SPICED PRESSED BEEF

4-lb. flank of beef (if salted, omit salt), remove superfluous fat.
Spice mixture—3 oz. salt, 1 oz. sugar, 1 teaspoon ground ginger, ½ teaspoon cayenne.
Vegetables—2 onions stuck with 2 cloves, bouquet garni, 2 carrots, scraped and sliced, 1 stick celery, sliced, 12 peppercorns.

Well rub surface of meat with spice mixture; leave for four days in cool place, turn frequently. Wipe meat and roll; cover with water, add vegetables and peppercorns, bring to the boil then simmer until slowly meat is shredding and there is very little liquid left in the saucepan. Drain. Press meat with a heavy weight. Serve cold and cut into thin slices.

POT-AU-FEU

1 *piece of beef skirt (or an inferior cut).* 1 *boiling chicken.* 2 *carrots, scraped and sliced.* 2 *large onions, peeled and sliced.* 1 *head of celery.* 4 *leeks, peeled.* 1 *small white cabbage, shredded.* 2 *turnips, peeled and sliced.* 1 *lb. potatoes, peeled. Seasoning of salt and pepper.*

Place chicken and beef in cold water, bring to the boil and skim well. Season and simmer for 1 hour. Add all the vegetables except potatoes; boil potatoes separately. Serve (per person) a slice of beef and a piece of chicken surrounded by the vegetables and potatoes. Accompany with Salsa Verde.

NECK AND CLOD

Juicy and good flavour.

BASIC WAYS OF COOKING

Stew, also use for meat puddings or pies.

STEAK AND KIDNEY PUDDING

1½ *lb. any stewing steak.* 8 *oz. kidney.* 4 *oz. mushrooms, washed and sliced. Worcester sauce.* 2 *large onions, peeled and chopped.* 1 *teaspoon cornflour. Chopped parsley. Seasoning of salt and pepper. Suet paste.*

Cut the meat and kidney in dice, place in saucepan, add onions and mushrooms. Cover with water, bring to the boil, skim. Season and simmer until three-quarters cooked. Add Worcester sauce and parsley to taste and thicken with diluted cornflour. Cook for further 10 minutes. Remove, allow to cool. (If desired ¼-bottle red wine may be added.) Line a pudding basin with suet paste, pour in the meat, cover with paste. Then cover with cloth and steam for 1½ hours. Serve pudding in the basin with napkin folded round it, standing on a dish.

LEG

Sinewy piece of beef.

BASIC WAYS OF COOKING

Stew, also use for mincemeat, soups or stocks and beef-tea. (Leg of beef and bones are wonderful ingredients for making stock, and a good stock may be used not only for soups but as a basis for sauces.)

BEEF TEA (Suitable for invalids)

1½ lb. leg of beef, or any lean beef, with fat removed and shredded very finely. Seasoning of salt. 1 pint water.

Place meat in a double pan; season, and cook slowly for 2 to 2½ hours. Skim thoroughly and strain.

CONSOMMÉ

3 lb. leg of beef (or any lean beef), finely minced and chopped. 1 celery heart, cut into small pieces. 4 carrots, scraped and diced. 1 leek, diced. 6 to-matoes, crushed. Seasoning of salt and 6 grains peppercorns. 1 onion, peeled and sliced. 1 gallon of stock or water. 4 egg whites and shells.

Mix together in a large pan-beef, celery, carrots, leek, tomatoes, seasoning, egg whites and shells, and add stock or water; mix very well. Place on the stove and bring to the boil, stirring frequently. Place on the stove or grill separately the thickly sliced onion until black on both sides, then add to the pan. (This will supply both colour and flavour.) When the consommé comes to the boil, do not stir any more. Remove from full fire, cover tightly, then allow to simmer for 3 hours *very slowly*. Strain thoroughly, preferably through a fine cloth. Re-boil and correct seasoning. May be served hot or cold or re-heated.

MINCED BEEF

Leg of beef, minced. 1 onion, peeled and minced. 1 tablespoon dripping or fat. 1 tablespoon flour. 1 pint water or stock. Slices of toast.

Melt the dripping in a saucepan, add flour, and brown. Add stock and bring to the boil. Add minced meat and onion ; cook for 2 hours slowly, or until liquid is reduced. If desired, 1 measure of sherry may be added before serving on toast.

RIBS AND WING-RIB

Cheaper roast than sirloin, lightly streaked with fat. Tender and juicy. Good family fare.

BASIC WAYS OF COOKING

Roast. Bones very good for stock, soup or gravy.

BONED AND ROLLED ROAST BEEF

Wing-rib, bone, trim, roll and tie. Seasoning of salt and pepper. Flour.

Season the meat and dust with flour; place on roasting-rack in roasting-tray. Roast in a hot oven for 10 to 15 minutes, then lower heat and continue roasting (25 minutes to lb., 25 minutes over).

Serve with gravy.

ROUND OF BEEF (TOPSIDE AND SILVERSIDE)

One side—topside; other side—silverside. Both reasonable joints.

BASIC WAYS OF COOKING

TOPSIDE (smaller type of joint). Boil, braise, roast. (Preferably braise, as inclined to toughen when roasted.)

SILVERSIDE (usually salted; creamy fat at the side; not bony so a boon to the large family. Boil, braise. (Wonderful joint to boil, for don't forget that silverside is responsible for the traditional "boiled-beef-and-carrots" dish !)

BRAISED BEEFSTEAK IN CIDER

Topside of beef, sliced. 1 bay-leaf. 1 sprig of thyme. ½ lb. onions, peeled and sliced. 1 clove of garlic. Cider.

Fry a few slices of topside for 5 minutes on either side. Put in a dish, cover with sliced onions which have been fried until tender ; then moisten well with cider. Add bay-leaf, thyme and garlic. Braise in a slow oven for 1 hour. Serve hot from the same dish.

CARBONADES OF BEEF À LA FLAMANDE

(A Belgian dish)

Topside of beef, sliced. 4 onions, peeled and minced. Seasoning of salt and pepper. ½ bottle of beer. Mixed herbs.

Lightly toss beef slices in butter or fat in a frying-pan, also lightly toss minced onion. Well layer a cocotte, cover with beef slices, then another layer of onions, season, and moisten with the beer. Add herbs. Cover tightly, and cook slowly in the oven for 2 hours. Serve hot.

BOILED BEEF AND CARROTS

Silverside of beef (if salted, soak in cold water overnight).

Put meat in a large pan and cover with water; bring slowly to the boil, then let simmer gently (20 minutes to the lb., 15 minutes over). Add prepared carrots sliced during last three-quarters-of-an-hour of cooking.
Serve on a hot platter with carrots and dumplings.

Alternatively, boiled beef may be served with Salsa Verde.

STEAKMEAT

Steakmeat includes chuck and bladebone. Reasonable and best cooked cut into large pieces rather than whole.

BASIC WAYS OF COOKING

Braise, brown stew.

BROWN STEW

2 lb. meat, cut into cubes. 1 lb. carrot, scraped and cut into cubes. 1 lb. onion, peeled and sliced. 2 cloves of garlic, chopped. 1 tablespoon flour. Seasoning of salt and pepper. 1 bouquet garni. 3 pints vegetable or meat stock, or water. 1 tablespoon tomato purée.

Shallow-fry meat and vegetables until brown, add flour, cook for a further 5 minutes. Add chopped garlic, tomato purée, and stock. Mix until smooth, add bouquet garni, season, bring to the boil, then let simmer for 1½ to 2 hours or longer according to the quality of the meat. When ready, skim well and correct seasoning. May be served with dumplings.

Wine or beer added to this stew gives the flavour a wonderful "zip"!

TOP RUMP

Smaller type of joint, like topside, but a little more fatty.

BASIC WAYS OF COOKING

Braise, roast, pot-roast (brown in pan with a little fat, vegetables and herbs—no liquid—added, tightly covered, and cook slowly until tender).

BEEF À LA MODE

Beef—top rump, topside, silverside, are the best cuts, but any piece of stewing beef will do if not too coarse. Grated nutmeg. 1 bouquet garni. 1 carrot, scraped and sliced. 1 onion, peeled and sliced. ½ bottle red wine. 1 tablespoon bacon fat. 4 cloves of garlic, crushed. Flour. ½ pint stock. 2 calves' feet, blanched. 12 button onions. 24 pieces of carrots and turnips, all shaped to the same size. Sprinkling of peas. Seasoning of salt and pepper.

Marinate the beef for at least 24 hours (longer, if possible) before cooking in the following manner :—
Rub beef with seasoning and a little grated nutmeg. Place in a basin, add bouquet garni, sliced carrot and onion. Pour over red wine. When ready to cook, drain beef and vegetables and keep the liquor. Put bacon fat into a deep saucepan or casserole, heat until smoking. Place in the beef, colour on all sides ; add sliced carrot and onion, bouquet garni and crushed cloves of garlic. Continue to fry for 5 minutes. Drain off surplus fat. Dredge with a little flour. Cook in the oven for 10 minutes. Remove. Add liquor and stock. Stir well, season. Add calves' feet. Cover and cook slowly for 4 hours. Remove the beef and feet. Strain the sauce, simmer slowly, skim well to remove all traces of fat. Place the beef in a casserole and surround with button onions and pieces of carrots and turnips which have

been previously shallow-fried for 2 or 3 minutes to give flavour. Pour on the sauce and cook until the vegetables are tender. Remove the beef. Slice thickly against the grain. Finely-shred the meat from the calves' feet. Place beef slices on a serving-dish, the shredded meat from calves' feet on top, surround with the vegetables, and pour over the sauce. Before serving, sprinkle with cooked peas. Generally served hot, but in summertime is wonderful as a cold dish, served with a salad and new potatoes.

If desired, tiny cooked mushrooms may be added as an extra garnish.

BEEF À LA CUILLÈRE

(A French speciality)

3 lb. beef—top rump, topside, silverside, or any good square thick piece of beef, even stewing beef, if not too coarse.

Toss beef with fat in a pan with prepared carrots and onions; moisten with $\frac{1}{2}$ pint white or red wine. Cover and cook very slowly for 4 to 6 hours or until meat is concentrated with the sauce.

Remove any grease before serving.

SIRLOIN

Expensive, superb and noble; therefore, with justification is it said that an English king of long ago "knighted" this meat "Sir Loin !"

Various terms or parts of sirloin

Baron of beef . . . . . double sirloin.

Tenderloin . . . . undercut of sirloin.

Contre filet de bœuf . .upper fillet of sirloin.

Fillet . . . . .cut from under part of sirloin.

Roast (best roasting part of beef). If cut into steaks—fry, grill, sauté.

ROAST BEEF

Use beef, 1st to 6th rib, sirloin or tenderloin. Potatoes, medium-sized, peeled. Seasoning of salt and pepper.

Wipe beef and rub with seasoning. Place, fat side up, in an open pan and start roasting in a hot oven to seal the meat. Sear for 20 minutes, then reduce heat to slow oven. (Allow 16 minutes to the lb. for rare beef, 22 minutes to the lb. for medium, 30 minutes to the lb. for well done beef.) Generally served underdone. Half-an-hour before meat is cooked, add potatoes under the beef, basting from time to time.
Carve the beef thinly against the grain, serve on heated plates at once, pour over the gravy.
Serve with horse-radish sauce and Yorkshire pudding.

ROAST BEEF GRAVY

Pour off the fat from the tray carefully so as to retain the beef juices. Place on the stove, re-boil and reduce to a glaze. Pour off the surplus fat. Add 1 pint stock (meat or vegetable), cook slowly. Reduce until desired quantity is obtained. Season and strain.

CONTRE FILET DE BŒUF

This is the upper fillet of the sirloin.

Roast. If cut into steakes—fry, grill. Wonderful roasted whole as "roast beef", see above, and served with stuffed aubergines, or stuffed capsicums, or marrows provençale, or stuffed tomatoes, or carrots vichy, or points of asparagus.

Another variation is contre filet de bœuf in the French manner, i.e., to lard it because it moistens the meat so favourably. This is done with fine strips of fatty lard passed right through the beef (every four inches) on a long larding needle. With the needle removed and the strips of lard inside, it makes a wonderful roast. Serve with brown sauce with the addition of one measure of sherry or madeira.

End of fillet may be used for the following recipes :

BEEF OLIVES

Fillet of beef, sliced thinly into wide strips spread with chopped onion and herb stuffing, rolled up and tied with cotton; then stewed gently in brown sauce or pot-roasted gently with pieces of orange rind.

BEEF STROGONOFF

12 oz. ends of fillet of beef, cut into fine strips. ½ oz. butter. 2 shallots, finely chopped. ½ pint cream, preferably sour or else "soured" with 1 dessertspoon vinegar. 1 measure sherry, if desired. Seasoning of salt and pepper. Chopped tarragon leaves.

Melt butter in *red-hot* frying-pan and allow to become *smoking hot*, add chopped shallots and cook until golden; add meat strips, season, and fry rapidly for 1 to 1½ minutes until browned both sides; remove meat to serving-dish. Pour sherry and cream into frying-pan and allow to thicken to desired consistency, add tarragon. Pour sauce over the meat and serve at once.

SAUTÉ BEEF CHASSEUR

1½ lb. fillet of beef, cut into small pieces. ½ lb. mushrooms, washed and sliced. 3 tomatoes, peeled and diced. 2 shallots, peeled and chopped. ¼ pint brown sauce. ¼ bottle white wine.

2 *cloves of garlic, finely chopped. Seasoning of salt and pepper. ½ teaspoon chopped tarragon leaves. Chopped parsley.*

Quickly shallow-fry the meat in butter until brown ; remove the meat, add shallots and mushrooms and toss until tender ; add white wine, tomatoes, brown sauce, and garlic. Season. Cook the sauce for 20 minutes. Remove. Add meat. Correct seasoning. Then add chopped tarragon leaves just before serving. If desired, chopped parsley may be added.

Hamburg Steak (see Remnants, page 36) and Steak Tartare (see Steaks, page 29) ; also suitable recipes for end of fillet of beef.

STEAKS

Deservedly, steaks have a chapter on their own ! And, if you do happen to come across that odd tough piece of steak, beat it well with a wooden spoon before use !

CHÂTEAUBRIAND

Very juicy thick slice (2 to 3 inches thick) in big end of beef fillet. Serves 2 to 4 people and is sliced into portions on the slant *after* cooking.

GRILLED CHÂTEAUBRIAND

Seal very quickly both sides under very hot grill and then cook slowly owing to its thickness.

CHÂTEAUBRIAND GRAND VATEL

Grill and serve with Béarnaise sauce.

CHÂTEAUBRIAND WITH OYSTERS
(Carpet bag steak)

Cut a Châteaubriand 1 lb. to 1 lb. 4 oz. in weight (serves 2), flatten, slit the side with a sharp knife, add 12 oysters; sew up the meat with string. Season with salt and pepper. Shallow-fry the steak in butter for approximately 20 minutes. Remove from the fire, take out the string, cut into slices.
Serve with its own juice.

FILLET STEAK

Trim fat and sinews before cooking.
Fry, grill, sauté.

And here is a healthy dish with fillet of steak which requires no cooking at all : —

STEAK TARTARE

Fillet of steak, nicely trimmed and all nerves removed, chopped very fine. 1 tablespoon each chopped onion, chopped hard-boiled eggs, anchovy fillets, capers, chopped parsley. Seasoning of oil, vinegar or lemon, salt, pepper and mustard. 1 raw egg yolk.

Shape and mix all ingredients together well. Serve nice and cold.

TOURNEDOS (FILET MIGNON)

Grill, sauté. May be garnished in numerous ways, i.e. with hearts of artichokes toppde with Béarnaise sauce—pimentos stuffed with rice—sliced mushrooms—stuffed aubergines—little bouquets. of vegetables arranged around the tournedos "à la Jardinière."

TOURNEDOS À LA BEAUGENCY

Toss tournedos in butter, serve on fried bread, cover with juice and top each tournedos with heart of artichoke filled with Béarnaise sauce with slice of poached beef marrow.

TOURNEDOS BÉARNAISE

Toss tournedos slices in butter, serve on fried bread, top with hearts of artichokes and Béarnaise sauce.

TOURNEDOS ROSSINI

Tournedos, trimmed of fat and sinews (1 per portion). Slices of goose liver, ¼ inch thick, rolled in flour. 12 thin slices of truffle. 1 cup brown sauce. 1 measure sherry or madeira. Seasoning of salt and pepper.

Sauté slices of goose liver on both sides in butter until golden brown. Sauté the tournedos in hot butter for 5 minutes each side and arrange on hot platter with slice of goose liver on top of each. (Keep hot.) Sauté truffle slices and sherry, stir in brown sauce, and cook until sauce is reduced two-thirds. Season and, if desired, stir in further 1 measure of sherry or madeira. Arrange truffle slices on goose liver and pour over the sauce. Serve immediately.

ENTRECÔTE
(Tenderloin Steaks)

Grill, fry. May be garnished with any seasonal vegetables or at hand, such as stuffed tomatoes, stuffed aubergines, stuffed marrows, etc.

You may obtain single or double entrecôte steaks ; therefore, if you require a whole steak for 2 portions, instead of cooking 2 separate ones, cook a double entrecôte and slice *after* cooking.

ENTRECÔTE BORDELAISE

Tenderloin steaks, well seasoned. 1 cup brown sauce. ¼ bottle red wine. 2 chopped shallots. Seasoning of salt and pepper.

Use a sauté-pan, not a frying-pan. Heat a little butter in the pan and cook the steaks rapidly on both sides. Remove. Add shallots to the pan, turn with a wooden spoon until cooked ; add wine and brown sauce ; simmer slowly for 10 minutes. Remove. Correct seasoning. Cover steaks with sauce.

MINUTE STEAK

Fry, grill. (From the sirloin.) This steak has to be well flattened which explains the reason for its name—it only takes a minute to fry or grill !

STEAK DIANE

Minute steak, well flattened out. 1 shallot or onion, peeled and chopped. Chopped parsley. Sprinkling of red pepper. Seasoning of salt, pepper and dash of Worcester Sauce.

Fry the shallot or onion in butter until golden, add minute steak and cook quickly on both sides ; add seasoning, chopped parsley and sprinkle with red pepper. Serve immediately. If desired, steak may be flambé with brandy.

PORTERHOUSE STEAK

Usually served grilled on fried bread. (This is a cut right across from the sirloin down to the fillet.) A lovely piece, tender and juicy.

RUMP STEAK

May be purchased as a joint, but generally takes the form of steaks. Expensive, but oh ! so lovely and tender. Rump steak should be cut 1 inch to 1¼ inches thick or else is inclined to curl and become dry when cooking ; its flavour may be enhanced by sprinkling very lightly with red pepper before grilling or by adding 1 measure of red wine or sherry or Madeira wine when frying.

POINT STEAK

This is the point surrounded by fat at the end of the slice of rump, generally considered much more succulent than any other steak.

MARROWBONE OF BEEF

A delicacy much appreciated on the Continent where they favour boiling a whole marrowbone, scooping out and eating the marrow meat with a spoon.

MARROWBONE CANAPÉ

(A tasty and unusual savoury)

Marrowbone meat sliced on toast with added savoury sauce (such as Bordelaise sauce), then placed under the grill for a minute.

SHIN (OX CHEEK)

Very reasonable, lean and tough, but nutritious.

BASIC WAYS OF COOKING

Excellent for brown stew, also for stock, soup, and for beef-tea. May be potted as well.

POTTED SHIN BEEF

Season with salt and pepper, pound with butter, and pot.
Alternatively : —
Chop very finely, season with mixed herbs, and egg and bread-crumb ; then fry in balls and serve with gravy.

OX TONGUE

A delicacy. (Usually purchased pickled.)

BOILED AND PRESSED TONGUE

(If taken fresh from the pickle, soak overnight.) Put into a saucepan of water and bring slowly to the boil, skim well, add prepared vegetables sliced, add mixed herbs, and simmer gently until cooked. (Try tip of tongue with a skewer to see if tender for, when tip is tender, the rest of the tongue *is* cooked !) Remove and skin immediately. Trim root a little, removing the bones. Roll tongue into a round and press into a large round cake tin. Place a board with weights on it on top, and leave overnight. When turned out it should be a nice compact round with a jellied surface.

OXTAIL

BASIC WAYS OF COOKING

Highly esteemed for soup. Also braise.

OXTAIL AUX HARICOTS

(If this dish is prepared the day before, its flavour is enhanced.)

Oxtail, cut in 2-inch sections (retain fine ends for making oxtail soup). 1 large onion, peeled and sliced. 1 carrot, scraped and cut in large dice. Flour. 3 cloves of garlic, crushed. 1 bouquet garni. 2 pints stock. 1 tablespoon tomato purée. 3 tomatoes, skinned and crushed. Haricot beans. ½ bottle red wine. Seasoning of salt and pepper.

Heat a little fat in a saucepan, place in oxtail, onion and carrot, shallow-fry until brown. Drain off surplus fat, add a little flour, mix well; add garlic and bouquet garni, cook for 10 minutes in the oven. Remove. Add stock, tomato purée, tomatoes, red wine, seasoning. Cook covered for 5 to 6 hours, slowly. Remove the oxtail. Skim well the sauce and simmer for 1 hour, removing all fat from time to time. Strain. Pour over the oxtail. Add haricot beans. (These may be dried beans soaked overnight and cooked without salt, or tinned baked beans.)

With oxtail ends make :—

OXTAIL SOUP

½ lb. oxtail ends, cut into small pieces. 1 carrot, scraped and diced. 1 large onion, peeled and diced. 2 or 3 tomatoes, peeled and chopped. 1 clove of garlic, crushed. 1 dessertspoon tomato purée. 1 bouquet garni. 1 dessertspoon flour. 2 pints stock or water. Seasoning of salt and pepper.

Fry oxtail pieces, carrot and onion in a saucepan until brown, add flour, cook in the oven for 10 minutes. Remove. Add tomato purée, chopped tomatoes, garlic, stock, and season. Cook slowly on the fire for 3 hours. Skim well. Strain. Recover the oxtail pieces and garnish the soup with them just before serving.

REMNANTS

With boiled beef left-overs :—

BEEF RECHAUFFÉ
Boiled beef left-overs, very finely chopped. 3 onions, peeled and finely sliced. 1 oz. butter. Seasoning of salt and pepper. Juice of ½ lemon. Chopped parsley.
Stew onions in butter until golden, add chopped beef, and season. When ready, garnish with parsley and sprinkle lightly with lemon juice.

With cooked beef or any cooked meat :—

HASH

Cooked meat, sliced. 1 oz. flour. 1 oz. butter. 1 onion, peeled and sliced. ½ pint stock. Seasoning of salt and pepper. 1 measure of sherry.

Melt butter in a pan, add flour and onion, cook until brown ; stir in stock, season, and cook for 5 minutes ; add sherry and meat and re-heat. *Do not boil.* Serve on toast.

SHEPHERD'S PIE

Cooked beef or any meat, minced. Dabs of butter or margarine. 1 onion, peeled and minced. Mashed potatoes.

Place minced meat and onion in a greased pie-dish, cover with mashed potatoes ; put the dabs of butter on top and bake in a moderate oven for ½ hour or until top is golden brown.

With raw beef left-overs :—

HAMBURG STEAK

1½ lb. raw beef, finely chopped. 6 (½-inch thick) slices of Spanish onion. 3 tablespoons melted bacon drippings. Seasoning of salt, pepper, and cayenne pepper. 3 tablespoons butter. 2 tablespoons grated onion. 1 tablespoon chopped parsley. 1 cup fresh bread-crumbs. 1 egg, well beaten. Slices of bacon.

Layer a greased or buttered baking-dish with onion slices, pour over them melted bacon drippings ; season ; cover tightly and bake in a moderate oven for 20 to 30 minutes. Meanwhile, melt the butter and stir in slowly grated onion, bread-crumbs and chopped parsley. Season, and add chopped beef, stirring continually. Remove from fire and work in this mixture with the beaten egg. Shape into 6 flat cakes and wrap each with a slice of bacon. Put each cake on each onion slice in the baking-dish and grill for 5 minutes each side ; baste regularly.

Serve on a hot platter garnished with chopped parsley. If desired, each Hamburg Steak may be topped with a poached or fried egg, or with a grilled tomato slice.

VEAL

In season all the year round, but more expensive in spring and winter.

Continental veal considered the best because it is milk fed only; thus, very tender and generally cooks very white.

Veal should be pale pink in colour and lean; any fat should be white and clear. Large overgrown veal is inferior to small delicate yet fat veal.

(Fillet of cow-calf is preferable to veal of bull-calf.)

BREAST

An economical joint.

BASIC WAYS OF COOKING

Braise, stew, bone and stuff and roll.

STUFFED BREAST OF VEAL (1)

1—4 lb. breast of veal, boned. 2 oz. butter. 2 onions, peeled and sliced. 2 carrots, scraped and sliced. Seasoning of salt and pepper. 1 cup boiling water. 1 cup cream. 1 tablespoon any meat extract (like Bovril). ½ cup Béchamel sauce.

Ingredients for stuffing : —

2 cups cooked rice, ½ cup sliced poultry liver sauté in butter. 1 tablespoon meat extract—mixed well together.

With a sharp knife, split open a "pocket" in the breast ; stuff, then sew edges together. Spread bottom of a casserole dish with butter, layer with carrots and onions ; season the breast and place on to the vegetable bed. Roast in a hot oven until browned, basting regularly. Add boiling water, cover the casserole, and continue cooking in the oven for 2 hours. When ready, remove veal to a hot platter. (Keep hot.) Add cream to vegetables in casserole dish, then cook on the stove, stirring continually, until cream reduced by half ; stir in meat extract and Béchamel sauce. Strain and serve this sauce separately.

STUFFED BREAST OF VEAL (2)

With a sharp knife, partially split open boned breast so as to enable meat to be rolled easily lengthwise ; spread sausage stuffing over the meat, roll up, wrap in a cloth and tie securely with string. Boil gently for 2 to 3 hours. Garnish with chopped parsley before serving.

The following is a delicious white stew :—

BLANQUETTE OF VEAL

2 *lb. veal, cut into dice (breast or shoulder).*
1 *large onion, peeled and sliced.* **12** *button onions.*
6 *button mushrooms.* **1** *oz. flour.* **1** *oz. butter.* **1**
*gill milk or light cream. Seasoning of salt and
pepper.*

Cover meat with water ; bring to the boil, skim ;
add large onion, season, simmer until nearly
cooked. Meanwhile, peel and boil button onions ;
peel and prepare mushrooms. Melt butter in a
pan, add flour and cook for 5 minutes. Add stock
from the meat, whisk well until smooth, cook
for 30 minutes. (Discard large sliced onion.) Then
add diced meat, button onions and mushrooms,
and simmer very slowly for 15 minutes ; add
milk or cream, correct seasoning.

SHOULDER

Generally divided into two ; the best piece—"oyster"—lies
towards the blade-bone.

BASIC WAYS OF COOKING

Braise, bone and roll and roast. Also suitable for stews and
pies. ("Oyster" is an excellent roast.)

ROAST SHOULDER OR NECK OF VEAL AND BACON

*1 large carrot, scraped and sliced. 1 large onion,
peeled and sliced. 4 leaves of sage. 1 pint stock
and water. 4 slices of bacon. 1 joint, boned (roll
and tie). Pinch of cornflour. Seasoning of salt
and pepper.*

Place vegetables in a tray plus the meat, season,

39

add the sage and roast for 40 minutes. Add stock and water. Cover and continue cooking until meat is tender. Remove. Skim well. Thicken stock lightly with cornflour. Cook for 10 minutes, strain. Slice the veal and pour over the sauce. Serve with a slice of grilled bacon.

Shoulder pieces may be used for :—
Blanquette of Veal (see Breast, page 39). Veal and Ham Pie (see Remnants, page 48).

KNUCKLE

Reasonable joint.

BASIC WAYS OF COOKING

Braise, stew, also used as pie meat.

OSSO BUCO MILANAISE

2 knuckles of veal. 1 dessertspoon tomato purée. 4 whole tomatoes, peeled and chopped. 1 bouquet garni. 1 large onion, finely chopped. 1 carrot, finely chopped. ½ bottle dry white wine. 1 piece of garlic, chopped. Seasoning of salt and pepper.

Request the butcher to saw through the knuckles in 2-inch sections. Flour the knuckles and shallow-fry in a saucepan until brown both sides ; add onion and carrots, cook for 5 minutes. Add white wine, tomatoes, tomato purée, bouquet garni and garlic, season, cover and cook slowly in the oven for 2 hours. When ready, remove the bouquet garni, transfer the meat to a hot platter and strain sauce over it.
Serve with Risotto Milanaise.

A fine white stock may be obtained from knuckle of veal or veal bones, as follows :—

VEAL STOCK

3 lb. knuckle of veal or veal bones. 2 quarts cold water. Seasoning of salt and pepper. 2 onions, peeled and sliced. 2 celery stalks.

Remove meat from bone and cut into small dice ; place meat pieces, bones, vegetables, water, in large pan and season. Allow to boil and skim regularly. Let simmer for 4 hours, then strain. *Veal bones are very good also for brown sauces of all kinds.*

LOIN

Loin chop is very tender ; loin roast has back-bone attached. End pieces of loin may be purchased quite cheaply.

BASIC WAYS OF COOKING

Bone and roll and roast, braise. If cut into chops—fry, grill, braise. May be roasted as roast shoulder (see "Shoulder," page 39).

ROAST LOIN OF VEAL

Wipe the boned joint, season with salt and pepper, stuff and sew up edges. Stand on a grid in a baking-tin and roast in a hot oven for 10 to 15 minutes, then lower heat and continue cooking in a moderate oven. Baste frequently. Should be well cooked and no blood should escape when cut. Serve with gravy and pass sage stuffing round separatey.

VEAL CHOPS AND CREAM

Shallow-fry the chops ; when ready, remove. Add cream to the frying-pan, season with salt and pepper, then pour this sauce over the chops.

VEAL CHOPS ALLA SASSI

4 veal chops (1 per portion), 2 oz. butter. 12 sage leaves. 24 new potatoes (if not available, use old potatoes shaped to new potato size). 1 measure of sherry. Seasoning of salt and pepper. Flour.

Flour the chops. Sauté 1 oz. of the butter in a sauté-pan, add chops and cook them quickly each side for 1 minute; add potatoes and sage, then place sauté-pan in a heated oven. Cook for 18 to 20 minutes, turning the ingredients regularly. When ready, remove chops, sage and potatoes to a hot dish. (Keep hot.) Meanwhile, drain fat from sauté-pan before adding sherry, cook for a minute on the stove, stirring continually, then pour sauce over the chops. Fry remaining 1 oz. butter until golden and also pour over the chops. Serve immediately.

BEST END NECK

Very good roast and in cutlets.

BASIC WAYS OF COOKING

Roast (see "Roast Shoulder or Neck of Veal," page 39), braise. If in cutlets—fry, grill, sauté.

VEAL CUTLET À LA MARIO

Veal cutlets (allow 1 per person), ¼ lb. Gruyère cheese. 3 tablespoons milk. 1 egg yolk. Egg and bread-crumbs.

Melt the cheese with milk, stir in egg yolk. Fry cutlets in butter, remove and allow to cool. Dip cutlets in the cheese mixture, then egg and bread-crumb the cutlets and fry in deep hot fat for 2 minutes. Serve with Madère sauce with the addition of a chopped truffle. Accompany with buttered zucchini, sautéd apple rings, and a bowl of tossed crisp green salad.

VEAL CUTLET PAILLARDE

Flatten the cutlet as thinly as possible, grill quickly both sides, and serve with lemon.

VEAL CUTLET SMITANE

Veal cutlets (from the leg also suitable). Season-ing of salt, pepper and ¼ teaspoon flour. 1 table-spoon butter. 2 cups Smitane Sauce. Grated Gruyère cheese.

Pound the cutlets, season; heat butter in a baking dish, put cutlets in and cook until both sides are browned. Remove them to buttered earthen-ware dish and pour Smitane sauce over them. Sprinkle with grated cheese and brown quickly under the grill.

LEG

A fine lean cut.

BASIC WAYS OF COOKING

Roast. If cut in thin slices—use for escallopes (flatten with a heavy knife or beat with a mallet or other wooden beater before cooking).

ROAST VEAL

1½ lb. leg of veal. 4 rashers of bacon. ½ cup cream. 1 cup stock. 1 tablespoon fat. 1 sliced onion. 1 sliced carrot. Juice of 1 lemon. Seasoning of salt, pepper, sage and rosemary.

Season the meat, place in a tray, add vegetables and fat. Roast for 30 minutes, add slices of bacon, cook for a further 10 minutes. Remove

joint and bacon, pour off the surplus fat, retain
sediment. Add stock, cream and lemon juice.
Reduce to half, correct seasoning. (Remember
that the salt from the bacon will salt the sauce
so taste before adding salt !) Slice the meat, strain
the sauce and pour over the meat, then lay bacon
on the top.

*The folowing is a fine hot weather dish because it may be kept for a few days in
the refrigerator until required.*

VITELLO TONNATO

*2 lb. boned leg of veal (skin and fat removed).
12 anchovy fillets. 6 oz. tunny fish in oil (tinned).
½ pint olive oil. ½ pint dry white wine. 1 bouquet
garni. Seasoning of salt.*

Make some incisions in the meat into which place
anchovy fillets, roll and tie with tape. Put meat
in a pan, add other ingredients, cover, and simmer
for 1½ hours on a low fire. Allow to cool, then
remove meat, pass sauce through a sieve. Stir
into a basin and add 1 cup thick cream and 1
teaspoon lemon juice ; season. Slice the veal and
pour over the sauce before serving. Garnish
with peeled and quartered tomatoes and slices
of lemon.

SALTIMBOCCA

*2 very thin and flattened slices of veal (per por-
tion), beef slices also suitable. 2 slices of ham
(per portion) and same size as veal slices. Fresh
sage leaves. Seasoning of salt and pepper. Butter.
1 measure of marsala or sherry. Fried pieces of
bread.*

Place slice of ham on to slice of veal and sage
leaf on to ham ; roll up and fasten with toothpick.
(Repeat this procedure according to the number
required.) Sauté in butter then add marsala.
Cook for a further 10 minutes. Serve on fried
pieces of bread.

Below are only several of the wonderful ways escallopes may be prepared :—

WIENER SCHNITZEL
(The Viennese speciality)

Veal escallopes (1 per portion), flattened as thinly as possible (also suitable if taken from the loin). Seasoning of salt and cayenne pepper. Flour. Egg and bread-crumbs. Butter or olive oil. Chopped parsley. Capers and olives. Slices of lemon. Anchovy fillets.

Season and flour the escallopes, egg and bread-crumb; sauté in hot frying-pan in butter until both sides are browned. Serve on a hot platter, each cutlet topped with a round slice of lemon, a rolled anchovy fillet and olive stuffed with capers. Garnish with chopped parsley.

Variations of Wiener Schnitzel :—

ESCALLOPE OF VEAL HOLSTEIN

Same as Wiener Schnitzel with the addition of a poached or fried egg on top of each cutlet, and with the slices of lemon, rolled anchovy fillets and olives stuffed with capers arranged around the hot platter instead. Garnish with chopped parsley.

ESCALLOPE OF VEAL NAPOLITAINE

Same as Wiener Schnitzel but serve with spaghetti and Napolitaine sauce.

With small pieces of veal left from the leg or the loin :—

SCALOPPINI AL MARSALA

Small squares of veal, sliced very thinly (4 squares per portion). Seasoning of salt, pepper and lemon juice. Flour. 2 oz. butter. 1 measure of marsala. 1 tablespoon stock.

Season and flour the veal squares. Melt butter in a frying-pan, add veal and cook quickly both sides ; add marsala, stir in stock ; cook for a further 2 minutes. Serve immediately with sauté mushrooms.

ESCALLOPE OF VEAL BEURRE NOISETTE

Escallopes of veal. Flour. Lemon juice. 1 tablespoon butter.

Flour the escallopes, fry quickly both sides, season, place on a hot platter. Skim fat from the pan, then add and melt butter until brown. Pour a few drops of lemon juice over the escallopes, cover with lightly browned butter, and serve at once. If desired, rosemary and sage may be sprinkled over the meat before the butter.

CALF'S HEAD

Preparation of calf's head for all recipes :—

CALF'S HEAD

Remove the outside flesh from the bone. Keep the tongue whole (or get your butcher to do this for you). Keep the brains whole. Place in a basin and keep under running cold water for 3 to 4 hours or let it soak overnight. For 1 head—take 1 dessertspoon flour, dissolve in ½ gallon water, add juice of 1 lemon and 1 dessertspoon salt, mix together until smooth. Bring head and tongue to the boil in plain water. Refresh. Cut into suitable pieces. Remove the ears and any hair. Place into the prepared water, bring to the boil, cover with a cloth and simmer until cooked.

CALF'S HEAD VINAIGRETTE

Prepare as above, serve on a hot platter with sliced tongue, and dress with Vinaigrette sauce.

CALF'S HEAD EN TORTUE

Cut hot meat and tongue into dice and heat slowly, *do not boil*, in the following sauce.

Sauce :—

2 cups calf's head stock. 2 tablespoons butter. 2 tablespoons flour. 2 chopped hard-boiled eggs. Seasoning of salt and pepper. 1 measure of sherry. 1 teaspoon chopped parsley.

Thicken stock with butter and flour, add eggs, season ; then add sherry and parsley.

Calf's ear may be used for hors d' œuvres in the following manner :—

Cut into fine strips, add an equal quantity of fresh capsicums cut in a similar manner, just a touch of garlic, a little chives or spring onions cut very fine, then mix together well with your favourite Vinaigrette dressing.

REMNANTS

Here is a pleasant "left-overs" dish which requires no cooking :—

VEAL MOULD

$\frac{1}{2}$ *lb. cooked veal (or any white meat or poultry). 1 pint veal or chicken stock. 1 hard-boiled egg, sliced. $\frac{1}{2}$ oz. powdered gelatine. Seasoning of salt and pepper. New carrots, scraped and finely grated. Chopped tarragon.*

Heat the stock, add seasoning and dissolved gelatine ; pour a little of the stock into a mould and set in the refrigerator. Chop the veal very finely, then put over the set stock in the mould; add egg. Gradually pour over rest of the stock and replace mould in the refrigerator (or in a cold place) to set. When ready, garnish with grated carrot and chopped tarragon.

A family favourite which is equally good hot or cold :—

VEAL AND HAM PIE

2 lb. cooked pie veal, cut into large pieces. ½ lb. gammon rasher, cut into thick shreds, boiled and drained. 4 hard-boiled eggs, quartered. Seasoning of salt and pepper. 1 egg, beaten. 1 tablespoon chopped parsley. Stock or water. Flaky pastry.

Fill a pie-dish with alternate layers of veal, gammon, eggs; season between the layers. Moisten well with stock. Roll out flaky pastry finely; brush edges of pie-dish with water; cut a strip of pastry to fit on and press round edge of dish. Cover whole dish with pastry, press down, and trim edges neatly. (Garnish centre with a flower-shaped pastry.) Brush with beaten egg. Wrap pie round with greaseproof paper and bake in a moderate oven for 1 hour.

Alternative method of making veal and ham pie is mentioned in Pork, page 54.

Left-over veal may be used for Blanquette (see Breast, page 39) or : —

CROQUETTES

Left-over cooked veal (or lamb or poultry) cut into small dice or minced. Cooked mushrooms, cut into small dice. Seasoning of salt and pepper. 2 tablespoons Béchamel sauce. 2 egg yolks. Flour. Egg and bread-crumbs.

Put well mixed veal and mushrooms into a pan with seasoning. Béchamel sauce and egg yolks; cook until mixture is blended and smooth; then spread on to a slab and allow to cool. Shape and cut with a large spoon, roll with flour, egg and bread-crumb, and fry in very hot fat. Serve with tomato or Madeira sauce.

HUNGARIAN GOULASH
(The wonderful Hungarian speciality)

2 or 2½ lb. cooked veal (or beef), cut into 2-inch cubes. 2 onions, peeled and finely sliced. Stock. 2 tablespoons butter. 2 tablespoons flour. Seasoning of salt, pepper and 1 dessertspoon paprika. 1 blade marjoram and 1 crushed clove of garlic. 1 cup sour cream.

Heat butter in a stew-pan, add onions and cook until golden brown; add meat, flour, seasoning, marjoram and garlic; stir in enough stock to cover; let simmer for ½ hour; add sour cream and cook for a further 5 minutes. If desired, 2 cups potato cubes may be added during last 15 minutes of cooking.

PORK

In season when there is an
"R" in the month, although
much better relished in winter
than in summer.
Pork is pink in colour. When
good, rind is thin, smooth and
cool to the touch; when too
long killed, it becomes flaccid
and clammy.
Sucking pig (piglet) also in
season when there is an "R'
in the month. Roasted whole.
A wonderful dish for a party
of 10 to 12 people.

BELLY

Economical piece.

BASIC WAYS OF COOKING

Salt and boil, braise. (Pieces suitable for flavouring pies, stews.)

PRESSED PORK

Wipe belly (already soaked in cold water to draw out salt) and place in a large saucepan well covered with water ; put on the lid securely and bring to the boil, then let simmer slowly until meat is shredding and there is very little liquid left. Drain. Press meat with a heavy weight. Serve cold and cut into thin slices.

BLADEBONE

Economical piece.

BASIC WAYS OF COOKING

Boil, bone and stuff and roast, pot-roast.

BOILED BLADEBONE

Wipe and season bladebone with salt and pepper ; place in large pan of boiling water with peeled and sliced onions ; cover and cook slowly for 1 hour approximately. (Add scraped carrots and turnips and peeled potatoes during last 20 minutes of cooking.)

HAND AND SPRING

A reasonable family joint.

BASIC WAYS OF COOKING

Salt and boil.

BOILED HAND

Salt and boil ; serve cold with pickled walnuts.

LEG

A large joint.

BASIC WAYS OF COOKING

Boil, roast (serve with apple or tomato sauce) and joint should be scored before roasting to give the crackling. Equally good served hot or cold.

ROAST PORK AU LAIT

2 lb. boned leg of pork (or loin), rolled with clove of garlic stuck inside. 2 pints warm milk. 2 oz. butter. Seasoning of salt and pepper. 2 small onions, peeled and chopped. 2 oz. ham, chopped.

Brown chopped onions and ham in the butter in a roasting-tray. Add seasoned rolled meat and brown it. Pour over warm milk. Roast in a moderate oven for 1 hour or until skin is golden brown and breaks. Pour sauce over the meat before serving. May be eaten hot or cold.

LOIN

Expensive fatty joint.

BASIC WAYS OF COOKING

Roast. If cut into chops—fry, grill.

ROAST PORK

Loin of pork. Seasoning of salt.

Wipe and season joint, place fat side up in roasting-tray; roast in a hot oven until fat or pork is sizzling, then lower heat and continue roasting in a moderate oven for 1½ to 2 hours. Should be *well cooked* and no blood should escape when cut. Serve with apple sauce.

GRILLED PORK CHOPS

Grill pork chops and serve topped with pineapple slices or with apple sauce.

PORK CHOPS CHARCUTIÈRE

Pork chops (or cutlets) grilled or fried, covered with devilled sauce with addition of sliced gherkins. Serve with mashed potatoes.

PORK CHOPS AU LAIT

Pork chops. Warm milk. Seasoning of salt, pepper, flour and pinch of thyme.

Season the chops, put in a baking-tin, pour in enough warm milk to cover ; bake in a moderate oven for 20 to 30 minutes.

SPARE RIBS

Small joint, leaner than loin and possesses a fair amount of crackling.

BASIC WAYS OF COOKING

Boil, roast. If cut into chops—fry, grill.(Chops are suitable for "barbecue" style cooking.)

BOILED SPARE RIBS

2 strips spare ribs, cut into sections. 12 peeled new potatoes (or 6 large potatoes, peeled and halved). 2 carrots, scraped and halved. 1 turnip, peeled and halved. Sauerkraut.

Put meat in a large pan of boiling water and let simmer for 1½ hours ; then add carrots, turnip, potatoes, and sauerkraut. Simmer for a further 20 minutes. Serve meat on a hot platter and decorate with the vegetables.

HEAD

A delicacy.

Salt and boil. Use for brawn.

BRAWN

1 pig's (or sheep's) head. 1 lb. knuckle of veal. Seasoning of salt and pepper, and nutmeg. Mixed herbs. Chopped parsley.

Pickle the head overnight; remove brains which are not needed for this recipe. Put head and knuckle in cold water to cover, bring to the boil, add seasoning and herbs, and let simmer for 3 hours or until flesh leaves the bones. (Skim regularly whilst cooking.) Remove meat from the bones and reduce the liquor until a jelly forms. When cold, cut up cooked flesh into small pieces together with the tongue; remove skin and gristle. Put into a wetted mould and strain liquor over it. Leave to set. When ready, turn out and garnish with chopped parsley.

REMNANTS

PORK PIE

1½ lb. cooked pork, cut into small pieces. Seasoning of salt and pepper. Short pastry. 1 teaspoon mixed herbs. 2 tablespoons water. ½ oz. gelatine. Stock, preferably from meat bones leftover. Beaten egg. Sprigs of parsley.

Line inside and bottom of greased pie mould with pastry. Mix thoroughly meat with seasoning and mixed herbs. Fill the mould with this mixture, then add water. Cover the mould with a pastry "lid," damp and secure the edges well. Make an incision in centre of the pie, brush all with egg, and bake for 2 hours in a moderate oven. Remove. Dissolve gelatine in stock and pour into the pie through the incision made in the pastry "lid." When set turn out, garnish with sprigs of parsley and serve cold.

Veal and Ham Pie may be cooked in similar manner.

PORK OR HAM SOUFFLÉ

Cooked pork left-overs (or ham) chopped. 1 oz. fat. 1 oz. flour. 2 eggs. ½ pint milk. Seasoning of salt and pepper. Chopped parsley.

Make a roux with the fat, flour and milk; add pork or ham and beaten egg yolks; fold in whisked egg whites, then pour into buttered soufflé dish. Bake bain-marie in a moderate oven for 20 to 30 minutes. Garnish with chopped parsley. Remember that a soufflé waits for no-one !

PORK STEW

1½ lb. cooked pork, cut into small cubes. 2 cups stock. 3 onions, peeled and boiled. 2 tablespoons fat (dripping or lard). Seasoning of salt, cayenne pepper, and mixed herbs. 1 tablespoon diluted cornflour.

Cook pork in fat until browned; stir in stock, season, bring to the boil, cover, and let simmer for 12 minutes. Add onions and diluted cornflour; bring to the boil, stirring continually. Correct seasoning. Serve with boiled sweet potatoes and a seasonal green salad.

BACON

Flesh should be clear red, without any yellow, rind thin, and fat firm and tinged red. Very dark bacon rind indicates salty bacon. "Green bacon" is unsmoked bacon. Gammon and Longback—delicious but expensive. Lean Collar—tender rashers and much cheaper. Collar or Slipper—good boiling pieces (weight $1\frac{1}{2}$ to $2\frac{1}{2}$ lb.).

BASIC WAYS OF COOKING

GAMMON AND LONGBACK. Grill and serve with devilled sauce (and broad beans when in season).

LEAN COLLAR. Fry.
COLLAR or SLIPPER. Boil.

BOILED BACON AND CABBAGE
(The classic tasty Irish dish)

Collar or slipper. Cabbages.

Soak collar in water overnight; place into a saucepan with sufficient cold water to cover, bring slowly to the boil, skim well, then simmer gently until cooked. Twenty minutes before bacon is cooked, place cabbages with it. When ready, strain thoroughly cabbages and serve finely chopped. This dish is usually accompanied by boiled potatoes. *Another way to serve boiled bacon :*—With mashed potatoes and pease pudding.

BACON PUDDING

4 oz. lean bacon. 4 potatoes, peeled. 1 large onion, peeled. 1 tablespoon chopped parsley, thyme, marjoram and sage. $\frac{1}{4}$ lb. suet paste or paste without fat. Seasoning of salt and pepper.

Roll out pastry; cut bacon and potatoes into dice, and mince onion. Spread all over pastry and sprinkle with the herbs and seasoning. Roll up, tie in scalded floured cloth and boil for 2 hours. To serve :—Turn out of cloth on to hot dish and surround with brown or tomato sauce.

CORNISH PASTIES

Short pastry, rolled out, ¼ inch thick.

Cut pastry into rounds, brush edges with water, spread filling on one half then fold over ; shape and press the edges. Bake in a moderate oven for ½ hour. For filling :—

> *Bacon, cut into small strips*
> 1 *teaspoon chopped parsley* } mixed together.
> 3 *beaten eggs*

Alternative filling :—

> *Minced steak*
> *Finely chopped onion* } mixed together.
> *Sliced potatoes*

HAM

Short thick ham preferable to long thin one. May be obtained fresh or smoked, but customarily obtained already boiled. Yorkshire, Hampshire, Westmorland, Suffolk, Norfolk, Devonshire, are the well-known English varieties, and York ham considered the best. Irish, Australian, Canadian, New Zealand, and U.S.A. (Virginia) hams good too.

BASIC WAYS OF COOKING

Boil, grill, braise, fry. (Americans favour ham cooked in cider.)

BOILED HAM

(If purchased uncooked)

Whole ham requires 24 hours' soaking before cooking to draw out the salt and pickle. Place in a saucepan with sufficient cold water to cover ; bring slowly to the boil, skim well, then after first 10 minutes simmer gently until done. (If cooked fast, ham toughens and falls to pieces.) Should be left in its own juice overnight. Remove, skin, and serve cold and sliced as and when required. How to serve : —Slice and serve with Madeira or sherry sauce. Blends well served with Purée of Spinach.

SMOKED HAM AND FIGS

Varieties—Parma, Bayonne, Westphalian, Ardennes, etc.

Arrange very thin slices of smoked ham (or coppa) on a dish with figs in the centre. (Allow 3 peeled figs per portion.) Serve very cold.

Ham remnants may be used for Ham Soufflé (see Pork Remnants, page 55), and for the following recipe :—

HAM MOUSSE

4 *oz. minced ham. 1 teaspoon gelatine. 1 cup tomato purée. 1 white of egg, stiffly beaten. ½ cup aspic jelly. 1 cup cream. Cochineal. Seasoning of salt and pepper. Chopped parsley.*

Place minced ham into a basin with the tomato purée, cream, seasoning and cochineal; dissolve gelatine in aspic jelly, add to the mixture. Fold in white of egg. Place in a mould and set in a cool place or refrigerator.

When firm, turn out and garnish with chopped parsley.

SAUSAGES (SAUCISSES)

Pork or beef. Pork considered the best.

BASIC WAYS OF COOKING

Fry, grill, bake, boil, poach. (When frying or grilling—if rolled in flour and pricked with a fork beforehand, they are less likely to burst and are more appetising.)

SMOKED SAUSAGE

Requires re-heating only.

BOLOGNA SAUSAGE
Needs no cooking.

DRY OR SUMMER SAUSAGE
Ready to serve.

FRANKFURTER SAUSAGE
Boil.

SAUSAGES AUX CHOUX
Grill or poach the sausages, and serve with braised cabbage.

FRANKFURTERS STRASBOURG
Boil the frankfurter sausages, and serve with braised sauerkraut.

SAUSAGES AU VIN BLANC
Fry sausages in butter, add 2 tablespoons white wine (or sherry) and serve on toast, pour sauce over. (If desired, serve with a Rice Pilaff instead of on toast.)

SAUSAGE GALANTINE
$\frac{3}{4}$ *lb. sausage meat. 1 onion, peeled and chopped. 1 beetroot, chopped. $\frac{1}{4}$ lb. grated carrots. 1 tablespoon chopped parsley. 2 tablespoons oatmeal. $\frac{1}{2}$ teaspoon sage. 2 eggs. Seasoning of salt and pepper.*

Mix well together all the ingredients in a basin but add and mix in eggs last. Put mixture into a greased baking-tin, cover with grease-proof paper and steam for $1\frac{1}{2}$ to 2 hours. Serve cold in slices with a seasonal salad.

The following is a favourite English breakfast dish :—

MIXED GRILL

Per portion :—
1 *sausage.* 1 *kidney, wash and skin.* 1 *chop.*
1 *rasher of bacon, remove rind.* 1 *tomato, halved.*
Seasoning of salt.

Heat the grill before placing together under it —
kidney, chop and sausage ; when nearly ready,
add bacon and tomato ; season to taste.

*Oddly enough, this recipe is often cooked by frying
in place of grilling ; in which case, follow the
same procedure but, instead, fry.*

TOAD-IN-THE-HOLE

1 *cup flour.*
1 *egg.*
1 *cup milk.* $\Big\}$ Batter.
$\frac{1}{4}$ *teaspoon salt.*
1 *lb. sausages.*

Place flour in a basin, season, add egg and beat
into a smooth mixture with the milk. Place
sausages in a greased pie-dish, pour over the
batter mixture, and bake in a moderate oven for
$\frac{3}{4}$ hour.

COTECHINO

(Italian speciality of Modena and Emilia which
may be purchased at any Italian or big provision
store).

Cotechino (large pork salame—weight 1 to 2 lb.).

Prick the sausage with a fork, place in a pan of
cold water lengthwise, and simmer slowly for 2
hours. Serve immediately, thickly sliced, with
lentils and mashed potatoes.

ZAMPONE DI MODENA

(Italian speciality of Modena which may be purchased at any Italian or big provision store)
1 *zampone (pig's foot, stuffed with cotechino
sausage mixture).*

Wrap in a cloth, place in cold water, bring to
the boil and simmer for 2 to 3 hours, according
to the size. Cut in slices, and serve with lentils
and mashed potatoes.

BLACK SAUSAGE

(This is a pork sausage including pork blood)
Fry sliced onions in butter until golden brown,
then add sliced black sausage, season to taste.

FEET (TROTTERS)

Calf's, pig's, sheep's. Calf's considered the best.

BASIC WAYS OF COOKING

Boil, grill, fry. (Calf's, pig's, sheep's feet, may be used in similar
manner.) Feet require blanching or slow boiling in salted water
before using, according to recipe; but customarily purchased
already boiled. Feet and bones are excellent, by the way, used
for a jellied stock.

BROILED FEET

Wipe and season the feet, place under the grill
for 5 to 10 minutes. Serve with Piquante sauce.

FRIED FEET

Wipe and season the feet, egg and bread-crumb,
then shallow-fry.

PIEDS POULETTE

Allow 3 calves' feet per portion. Remove the
hooves with the point of a knife, split the leg in

two lengthwise, break off the top bones, and soak for 3 hours or overnight.

Cook in salted water to which lemon juice and 1 dessertspoon flour per quart has been added. When tender, allow to cool, then remove all pieces of remaining bones.

For the sauce :—1 pint stock or milk (chicken stock is best but milk may be used instead). ½ oz. butter. ½ oz. flour. 1 egg yolk. 1 tablespoon cream. Seasoning of salt and pepper.

Cook butter and flour together without colouring for 5 minutes ; add boiling stock, whisk well until smooth ; season and cook for 30 minutes slowly. Remove from the fire, strain, beat egg yolk and cream together, add to the sauce whisking rapidly. *Do not re-boil.* Add the calves' feet. If desired, button mushrooms and small onions may be cooked and added.

Calves' feet may also be served hot with vinaigrette sauce.

OFFALS

BRAINS

Lamb's, sheep's, calf's.

BASIC WAYS OF COOKING

Boil, grill, poach, sauté. (Before cooking, soak in salted water with ½ teaspoon lemon juice or vinegar, rinse well and skin.)

POACHED BRAINS

Poach brains with Court Bouillon, drain, serve with Beurre Noir, sprinkle with capers and garnish with chopped parsley.

PARBOILED BRAINS

Cook in salted water, bring to the boil, then stand on the side of the stove for 10 minutes. Drain. Serve with Beurre Noir and garnish with chopped parsley.

SAUTÉ BRAINS

Sauté in butter with a few drops of lemon juice. Garnish with chopped parsley before serving.

SCALLOPS OF BRAINS

Place in a dish cooked slices of scallops of brains, add some rasped Gruyère cheese, cover with Béchamel sauce, sprinkle with bread-crumbs, top with a knob of butter, and grill.

BRAINS À LA YORK

Calf's brains, boiled. ¼ lb. mushroom caps, peeled and sliced. Seasoning of salt and pepper. 1 cup White Sauce (thick). 1 measure of sherry.

Press brains under weight ; cut into dice. Add sherry, cover, and allow to stand for 1 hour. Sauté mushrooms, then add to White Sauce. Add brains, season, and cook for 5 minutes.

63

HEARTS

Beef's, calf's, pig's, sheep's, lamb's. Calf's considered the best. Nutritious but not so tender as liver or kidneys ; therefore, have to be cooked much more slowly.

Calf's heart serves two portions. Beef's heart serves four portions. Sheep's heart serves two portions.

BASIC WAYS OF COOKING

Bake, boil, braise, sauté, roast (serve with redcurrant jelly).

BOILED HEART

Clean hearts, then let simmer in water until tender. Split and remove gristle. Chop. Season and serve on toast garnished with chopped parsley.

SAUTÉ HEART

Clean and wash ; finely slice, then soak for 2 hours in cold salted water ; sprinkle with bread-crumbs and sauté in butter for 15 minutes.

STUFFED SHEEP'S HEART

2 hearts. Veal stuffing (see Stuffings, page 182). 2 knobs of dripping. Chopped parsley (or sprigs of watercress).

Wash hearts and stuff with veal stuffing ; place dripping on each ; put in a casserole dish and bake in a moderate oven for 1 hour. Serve with gravy, and garnish with sprigs of watercress or chopped parsley.

And, finally, a traditional dish which—every Scot will agree—has a heart!

HAGGIS (Sheep's)

Sheep's stomach bag. Pluck (heart, liver and lights). ½ lb. minced beef suet. Seasoning of salt and pepper. 1 cup toasted oatmeal. 4 onions, peeled and parboiled. 1 pint pluck boilings.

Wash bag in cold water, scrape and clean well, soak overnight in salted water. Wash pluck, place in a pan of boiling water, boil for 2 hours with wind-pipe hanging out. Allow to cool, then cut off wind-pipe. Grate a quarter of liver only (remainder not needed for haggis) and mince heart, lights, onions and suet; add oatmeal, seasoning, and 1 pint stock in which pluck was boiled. Mix well together, fill bag more than half full of this mixture; sew up, and place in boiling water. Boil for 3 hours and prick at intervals so as to prevent bursting.

KIDNEYS (ROGNONS)

Beef's, veal's, lamb's, mutton's. (Mutton kidneys considered rather indigestible.)

BASIC WAYS OF COOKING

Braise, fry, grill, sauté, stew. (Need skinning after washing or soaking in salted water with teaspoon lemon juice.)

KIDNEYS SAUTÉ AU MADÈRE

1 lb. veal or lamb kidneys. 2 tablespoons brown sauce. 1 large glass madeira. 4 oz. mushrooms. 1 oz. butter. Seasoning of salt and pepper.

Cut the kidneys into 4. Cut the mushrooms into 4 or 6. Wash well. Shallow-fry the kidneys and mushrooms quickly. Remove. Re-heat the pan, add madeira, then the brown sauce, season. Cook for 5 minutes. Remove from fire, add kidneys and mushrooms, and work in 1 oz. butter. Do not re-boil. Serve with fried snippet of bread.

KIDNEYS SAUTÉ AU VIN BLANC

2 calf's kidneys, trimmed and sliced thinly. Melted butter. Seasoning of salt and pepper. 1 oz. chopped shallots. 1 gill dry white wine. 1 gill brown sauce. Sprinkling of chopped parsley. Knob of butter.

Flour kidney slices, and toss for 3 or 4 minutes in melted butter over a low heat. Season. Remove from frying-pan and place in a casserole dish. In the frying-pan, fry chopped shallots, using same butter as used for kidneys. When shallots are soft, add white wine and boil for 5 minutes. Then add brown sauce, stir well and pour this sauce over the kidneys. Heat for 5 minutes, BUT DO NOT BOIL, and serve immediately with chopped parsley and knob of butter.

KIDNEYS BROCHETTE (1)

Slit kidneys in half yet do not separate; skewer, grill, and serve with Maître d'Hôtel Butter in the centres.

KIDNEYS BROCHETTE (2)

Kidneys, trimmed. Slices of bacon. Mushrooms caps. Seasoning of salt and cayenne pepper. Brown stock. Pieces of toast.

Slice the kidneys, then arrange alternate slices of kidney and bacon on skewers with mushroom cap at each end. Broil and serve on toast, covered with stock sauce and seasoned.

KIDNEYS TURBIGO

Kidneys, cut into 4. Chipolatas (4 pieces per portion). 1 large mushroom, cut into 8 pieces. 1 tablespoon butter. 1 knob of butter. 1 measure of madeira. 1 cup brown sauce. Seasoning of salt and pepper. Heart, chopped. Fried pieces of bread.

Sauté kidneys in butter rapidly ; remove kidneys, add chipolatas and mushroom pieces ; sauté, then add madeira and brown sauce. Replace the kidneys, DO NOT RE-BOIL, and work in knob of butter ; correct seasoning. Serve with chopped heart on fried pieces of bread.

KIDNEY SOUP

½ lb. ox kidney. ¼ lb. lean meat, cut into small pieces. 1 carrot, 1 onion, 1 turnip. Seasoning of ¼ teaspoon salt. 1 celery stalk. 1 quart water. 1 oz. fat. 1 oz. flour.

Heat fat, fry the kidney and meat pieces. Remove from pan and brown vegetables and flour. Add water, season ; add meat. Let simmer for 1½ hours. Remove three-quarters of the kidney pieces and pass the remaining quarter through a sieve. Garnish with kidney pieces and serve immediately.

LIVER

Beef's, calf's, lamb's, pig's. Select liver with hardly any odour and of a bright red colour. Calf's liver is considered the best.

BASIC WAYS OF COOKING

Braise, broil, sauté, fry, bake with bacon. (Should be cut into slices or strips or diced before cooking.)

FRIED LIVER

Soak liver in milk. Then slice and shallow-fry for 4 to 6 minutes. Do not over-fry as best underdone. Serve with fried bacon and onions.

LIVER JOSEPHINE

(This is a very appetizing dish.)

1 lb. liver, diced. 1 large onion, peeled and sliced. Seasoning of salt and spice. ½ cup tomato purée. 1 cup stock or water. Sprinkling of flour.

Fry onion in butter or fat for 5 minutes ; sprinkle diced liver with flour and add to the onion ; season, add tomato purée and stir in stock. Let simmer for 10 minutes.

RAGOÛT OF LIVER

1 lb. calf's liver, sliced. 1 onion, peeled and sliced. 1 carrot, scraped and sliced. 1 oz. butter or fat. 1 dessertspoon chopped parsley. ½ teaspoon thyme. 1 bay-leaf. 1 tablespoon lemon juice. Seasoning of salt. ½ cup cream, sour preferable. 1 tablespoon bread-crumbs.

Melt butter in casserole dish, add onion, carrot, parsley, thyme, bay-leaf. Add liver and lemon juice, season, and cook on the stove for 10 minutes. Then add cream and bread-crumbs and continue cooking slowly until liver is tender.

SWEETBREADS (RIS DE VEAU)

Thymus glands of calf. A great delicacy.

BASIC WAYS OF COOKING

Braise, broil, fry, sauté. (Soak sweetbreads in running cold water for 12 hours before use to remove all traces of blood. Then place in cold salted water, bring to the boil, refresh, and use according to recipe.)

BROILED SWEETBREADS

Parboil, split, season with salt and pepper, and grill for 5 minutes. Serve with Beurre Noir or Maître d'Hôtel Butter.

SWEETBREADS AU SHERRY

4 sweetbreads. 1 tablespoon stock. 2 measures of sherry. 2 tablespoons brown sauce. 2 onions, peeled and sliced. 2 carrots, scraped and sliced. 1 bouquet garni. Seasoning of salt and pepper.

Place sweetbreads in a pan of cold water, bring to the boil. Cool, and remove all fat and sinews from the sweetbreads. Place in stewjar on a bed of onions and carrots, add bouquet garni, stock, and season. Cover tightly and cook slowly in the oven for 1 hour. Remove. Add sherry and brown sauce. Cover and cook for 30 minutes. Remove the sweetbreads. Place on a serving dish. (If desired, add 2 slices of truffle per sweetbread.) Strain the sauce, re-boil, simmer slowly, remove carefully any traces of fat, correct seasoning, and pour over the sweetbread.

SWEETBREADS MARÉCHALE

2 large sweetbreads. Point of asparagus, boiled. Bread-crumbs. Melted butter.

Place the sweetbreads in a pan of cold water, bring to the boil. Cool, and remove all fat and sinews from the sweetbreads. Cut into slices ½ inch thick, bread-crumb and shallow-fry. When ready, garnish with points of asparagus and, before serving, pour over a little melted butter.

SWEETBREADS SOUVAROFF

4 sweetbreads. Diced truffle. Diced foie gras. 1 measure of sherry.

Braise the sweetbreads, then put in a cocotte, add truffle and foie gras, add sherry ; cover with the lid, bake in the oven for 5 to 10 minutes. Not more.

TRIPE

The muscular wall of the first and second stomachs of beef. Honeycomb tripe considered the best.

BASIC WAYS OF COOKING

Boil, broil, stew.

TRIPE AND ONIONS

2 lb. tripe, cut into 3 inch squares. 6 onions, peeled and sliced. Water to cover. 1 quart milk. ¼ lb. butter. 1 tablespoon flour. Seasoning of salt and pepper. 1 tablespoon cream.

Place tripe and onions in a saucepan; cover with water and blanch; strain, pour milk over and boil for 1 hour or until done. Put in another saucepan—butter and flour, cook for 3 minutes. Pour milk from tripe into it and mix well. Cook for 10 minutes, season, and then mix with the tripe; add cream and serve immediately.

TRIPE MILANAISE

1 lb. tripe, wash, dry, and cut into very fine strips. 2 tablespoons oil. 4 tomatoes, peeled and chopped. 2 onions, peeled and shredded. 1 clove of garlic, chopped. Seasoning of salt and pepper. Chopped parsley.

Heat oil in a pan, add tripe and onions and sauté. Cook for 20 minutes, then add tomatoes, garlic, seasoning; cover, and cook for 10 minutes. Sprinkle with chopped parsley before serving.

TRIPES À LA MODE DE CAEN

3 lb. fresh honeycomb tripe, washed and drained, then cut into wide "finger" strips. Foot of beef, separated into two. Fat salt pork. Vegetables—4 onions, peeled and sliced; 4 carrots, scraped and

*diced ; 2 leeks ; 2 celery stalks. Herbs—1 tablespoon
minced chervil ; 2 bay-leaves ; 6 grains of peppercorns ; ½ teaspoon each thyme and marjoram.
Seasoning of salt and Cayenne pepper. ½ pint
cider. 1 measure of brandy. Chopped parsley.*

Layer bottom of casserole dish with fat salt pork,
then vegetables, followed by tripe ; add beef foot,
herbs and seasoning ; moisten with cider and
brandy. Cover very tightly and securely and
bake in a slow oven for 10 hours. Garnish with
chopped parsley before serving.

BASIC METHODS OF COOKING MEATS

BOIL

(This method is suitable for larger rather than small joints.) Joints for boiling should be tied securely with string ; place fresh meat into boiling water, bring back to the boil, then simmer until tender.

When boiling beef, try to "skewer" a hole into the joint and fill with a clove of garlic ; it not only enhances the flavour of the meat but also the stock.

Salt Meat—requires 24 hours' soaking ; place into tepid water and bring slowly to the boil, then simmer until tender.

BRAISE

Cook slowly, tight-covered, in a small quantity of liquid at a low temperature in the oven.

DEEP-FAT or FRENCH FRY

Cook in hot fat deep enough to cover food lowered in wire basket. When delicately brown, drain on unglazed soft paper or paper towelling. Never allow fat to remain in deep pan after using ; strain, then pour into a clean container for future use.

FRY

Unless meat is minced and protected in batter, meat should always be "dry" fried in a frying-pan, i.e., fried in a small quantity of fat or butter.

FRICASSÉE

Stew of white meat or poultry, served in white sauce.

GRILL or BROIL

(This method is suitable for cutlets, steaks, chops, kidneys, etc.).

Wipe meat, trim off surplus fat, season and brush over either with oil or melted fat. See that the grill is hot before placing meat underneath on a greased grid. Cook quickly to seal, turn—with 2 spoons, 2 knives or tongs but do not prick with fork—and cook other side. Allow 10-15 minutes for steak according to thickness, 10 - 20 minutes for chops, 6 - 8 minutes for cutlets, approximately 8 minutes for kidneys. Either moisten dish with fat and juice from meat or serve with Maître d'Hôtel butter (parsley, lemon juice and butter blended together).

POT-ROAST

Similar to Braise, except that the cooking may be in oven *or* on top of range.

ROAST

(When roasting beef, lamb, mutton, pork, veal, fat must not be put on the meat.)

Wipe meat. Stand on a grid in a baking-tin and roast in a hot oven for 10 - 15 minutes, then lower heat and continue cooking in a moderate oven. Baste frequently. Cooked meat springs back when pressed gently with finger. Pork or veal should be well cooked and no blood should escape when cut.

Any roast meat straight from the oven is inclined to be taut ; therefore it improves if kept hot (hot-plate or oven) and is allowed to settle and "relax" at least 10 - 15 minutes before carving.

SAUTÉ

Same as "Shallow-fry" but shake the pan constantly.

SEAR

To subject to intense heat in order to seal in juices.

SHALLOW-FRY

Cook in small quantity of fat, then turn over and cook on other side ; lower heat and cook slowly until done.

SIMMER

Cook just below boiling-point, on top of the stove.

SKEWER

To keep a piece of meat, etc., in shape for cooking by fastening together with a thin pointed rod or pin of wood or metal.

STEW

Cook slowly, tightly covered, in a small quantity of liquid at low temperature.

POULTRY AND GAME

Poultry and game should be
plucked, cleaned and trussed
before cooking unless
otherwise stated.
All roast game-birds may be
served separately with gravy,
browned bread-crumbs,
and bread sauce, and garnished
with watercress and game
chips (hot potato crisps).
Red game, generally, is best
during frosty weather.

CHICKEN

In season all the year round. When young, legs and combs are smooth ; when old, rough. Should be plump on breast, fat on back and have pliable feet.

Baby chicken (poussin) in season all the year round. By the way, baby chicken is so tender and succulent that it cooks quickly ; therefore, from my point of view, it is best either roasted in butter with a sprig of rosemary, or split and grilled. Roast, grill—15 to 20 minutes' cooking time.

BASIC WAYS OF COOKING

Boil, braise, broil, fricassée, fry, roast, stew.

BOILED CHICKEN

Clean and wash boiling chicken ; place in a pan of cold water, bring to the boil, skim, season, and simmer until tender.

GRILLED CHICKEN

Clean chicken, cut down side of the backbone, beat flat ; remove backbone, season, paint with oil or fat ; place under grill and cook, turning over from time to time, until tender.

TO PREPARE CHICKEN FOR ROASTING

Have chicken cleaned by your butcher but retain liver. If you wish to clean it yourself, cut off neck near the body. Separate neck from head by pulling apart. Cut off feet. Slit lower abdomen with the point of a knife and remove stomach, heart, liver and lungs. Throw away lungs and intestines.

With liver of poultry you can make the delightful Liver Stuffing (see page 181).

ROAST CHICKEN

Put fat on top of chicken and spread on the breast. Cook in a very hot oven for 10 to 15 minutes, then lower heat for remainder of the time. Cook for $\frac{1}{2}$ hour to 1 hour, according to size.

If you wish to utilize your chicken in several ways, then the following shows how each piece may be cooked :—

When chicken is cleaned, cut through meaty part of stomach and peel off. Remove chicken legs. Remove wish-bone. Take off breasts. We now have :

2 *breasts (wings).* 2 *legs. Liver.* 1 *carcase (stomach, neck, heart, feet).*

With chicken wings :—

CHICKEN MARYLAND

2 *chicken wings (breasts).* 1 *peeled banana.* 2 *tablespoons tinned sweet corn.* 2 *slices of bacon.* 1 *egg yolk.* 2 *small tomatoes, peeled.* 1 *sprig of parsley, fried. Hot Horse-radish sauce. Breadcrumbs.*

Skin the wings and bread-crumb.
Split the banana, pass through flour, egg wash. Grill tomatoes and bacon. Deep-fry chicken, corn fritters, and banana slices. Dress chicken with bacon and tomatoes, garnish with banana and fried parsley. Serve with sweet corn fritters and pass hot Horse-radish sauce round separately.

HOT HORSE-RADISH SAUCE

Grate 1 tablespoon horse-radish, place in small saucepan, add 1 tablespoon cream, cook slowly until mixture thickens, remove and keep hot.

SWEET CORN FRITTERS

Reduce sweet corn on the stove until nearly dry, add egg yolk, mix very quickly and thoroughly ; when cold, turn out on a plate, divide in two, shape into croquettes and bread-crumb.

CHICKEN À LA KING

2 chicken wings (breasts). ½ pint thick cream. Seasoning of salt and pepper. 2 oz. tinned red peppers. 1 oz. butter. 1 slice of toast per portion.

Skin wings, then cut into 1 inch pieces. Heat butter in small saucepan; add chicken, cook quickly for 2 minutes; add diced peppers and cream. Season. Cook for 10 minutes. Serve at once on toast.

With chicken legs :—

GRILLED LEG OF CHICKEN DEVILLED

2 chicken legs. 2 tomatoes. 2 slices of bacon. Fat or oil. 4 oz. mushrooms, peeled. Seasoning of salt and pepper.

Season legs well, paint with fat or oil, grill for 10 minutes each side. Remove. Well wash mushrooms; place mushrooms and whole tomatoes in a dish with the chicken legs and cook in the oven for 10 minutes. Remove. Dress each leg with grilled bacon before serving.

CHICKEN SAUTÉ

2 chicken legs. 1 tablespoon oil. 1 chopped onion. 2 tomatoes, peeled and diced. 4 oz. peeled, washed and sliced mushrooms. 1 piece of garlic, crushed and finely chopped. Chopped parsley (well washed and dried before chopping). 1 pint brown sauce. Seasoning of salt and pepper.

Heat oil in a saucepan. Divide chicken legs in two by cutting through the knee joint. Fry legs until brown, add onion. Add mushrooms and tomatoes, cook rapidly for 5 minutes, then add garlic. Strain off any surplus oil, add Brown sauce, bring to the boil. Season. Simmer slowly for 45 minutes, skimming well from time to time. Add plenty of chopped parsley before serving.

Turkey winglets may be used instead of chicken legs.

With chicken liver : —

If not used for other purposes mentioned, the livers may be used for breakfast with scrambled eggs or fried eggs. Remove bile carefully (if this is broken it will render livers bitter and inedible). Cut into small pieces, season with salt and pepper, shallow-fry quickly in a little hot fat and serve with eggs scrambled or fried, as desired.

Alternatively, use for Omelette au Foie de Volaille or Œufs sur le Plat. (See Eggs, page 211).

With chicken carcase : —

CHICKEN SOUP

Carcase (stomach, neck, heart, feet, giblets, etc.). 1 onion. 1 small leek. 1 carrot. 2 or 3 parsley stalks. Seasoning of salt and pepper. 2 oz. margarine. 1 oz. flour. 2 pints water. ¼ pint thin cream.

Place chicken carcase, etc., in a saucepan, cover with cold water, bring to the boil. Place under cold top and wash well. Replace in saucepan, add 2 pints water, bring to the boil again. Peel onion and carrot, wash well leek and parsley stalks and slice roughly ; add to chicken, season. Cook slowly for 45 minutes, then strain off the stock. Remove all meat from the carcase and cut into small dice. Cook together margarine and flour for 5 minutes, stirring continually, but

do not colour. Remove from stove, whisk in the
stock and stir until smooth. Season. Bring to the
boil and simmer for 30 minutes. Strain. Add
cream and diced chicken. Serve with snippets of
bread quickly fried or toasted.

CHICKEN BROTH

*Chicken carcase, etc. 1 carrot. 1 onion. 4 sticks
celery. 6 sprigs of parsley, coarsely chopped.
1 oz. pearl barley, well washed. Seasoning of salt
and pepper. 3 pints water.*

Bring carcase, etc., to the boil in plenty of water ;
then place under cold tap and wash well. Re-boil
in fresh water, add barley. Prepare all vegetables
cut into fine dice or pass through mincer (coarse-
plate) and add to stock. Cook for 1 hour. Strain,
and continue to cook slowly for 1 hour. Season.
Add chopped parsley before serving.

With chicken consommé or broth make :—

STRACCIATELLA

*1½ pints good chicken consommé. 2 oz. grated
Parmesan cheese. 2 eggs.*

Bring the consommé to the boil. Beat the eggs
and grated cheese together, add to the consommé.
Whisk well and serve at once.

*Chicken stock and chicken liver may be used
for Risotto Milanaise (see page 186).
With left-over pieces generally :—*

VOL-AU-VENT OF CHICKEN RÉGENCE

Left-over pieces or legs of chicken may be used
in this recipe.

*Chicken left-overs, cut in ½ inch dice. 12 button
onions, peeled and cut in 4. 6 white mushrooms.*

¼ *pint milk. 2 tablespoons cream. 2 oz. butter.*
Cornflour. Seasoning of salt and pepper.

Melt the butter in a saucepan, add onions and
mushrooms, cover and cook slowly for 10 minutes. Add the chicken and milk, cover and cook
for 45 minutes slowly; thicken lightly with cornflour and cook for 5 minutes. Add cream and
correct seasoning.

Serve in hot pastry cases which can be an outside
purchase, or made as follows :—

Roll puff paste ½ inch thick, cut with a 4 inch
round cutter. Make another cut on the same
piece of paste with a 3 inch cutter. Not too
deep. (Cutters may be purchased which give
the 2 cuts in one operation.) Egg-wash. Stand
for 15 minutes. Place on a greased tray. Bake
for 15 minutes in a hot oven.

CHICKEN CUTLETS

4 oz. chicken left-overs, finely chopped. 1 table-
spoon cream. ½ oz. flour. 1 cup white bread-crumbs.
2 eggs. ¼ oz. butter. Seasoning of salt and pepper.
Fried parsley.

Place butter in a saucepan, heat, add chicken.
Cook quickly for 2 minutes on a hot fire; add
flour, mix well together; add cream, season.
Cook for 5 minutes. Add yolk of one egg and
mix well together. DO NOT RE-BOIL. Remove
from stove and allow to cool, then shape into
cutlets. Beat remaining egg and egg white
together, pass cutlets in flour and into egg;
bread-crumb, pat with a knife and shallow-fry
until brown. Serve immediately garnished with
fried parsley.

If you wish to prepare chicken in other ways,
try the following recipes :—

CHICKEN WATERZOIE

(A Flemish speciality.)

1 *chicken, preferably a roaster*. 1 *leek*. 2 *onions*. 1 *head of celery*. 1 *oz. butter*. ½ *oz. flour*. 2 *egg yolks*. 1 *gill cream. Seasoning of salt and pepper*.

Clean the chicken, wash, dry well, remove the legs and cut each in two, remove the wings, cut off the breast and divide in two (giving 1 piece of white meat and 1 leg per portion). Wash vegetables and cut into fine strips; peel and shred onions. Melt half the butter in a saucepan and add chicken; fry lightly without colouring for 5 minutes, add all vegetables and cover tightly and cook slowly for 10 minutes. Add 1½ pints water and season; cook for a further 20 minutes. (If a boiling fowl, allow longer cooking time.) Strain off the stock, and keep chicken hot.

Meanwhile, melt ½ oz. butter in a saucepan, add flour and mix well. Cook for 5 minutes without colouring and stirring continually. Remove from fire and add the stock, whisk until smooth, then return to fire and cook slowly for 30 minutes; mix egg yolks and cream together and add to boiling stock, whisk well and remove from heat. DO NOT RE-BOIL. Pour over the chicken and serve immediately.

FRICASSÉE OF CHICKEN

1 *chicken (roaster)*. 6 *white mushrooms (each cut in 4)*. ½ *bottle dry white wine. Seasoning of salt and pepper*. 16 *button onions*. ½ *pint cream*. 1 *oz. butter*.

Clean the chicken, remove the legs, divide in 2. Cut off the 2 wings and cut the breast in 2. Heat the butter in a stew-pan. Place in the chicken and lightly colour, turning each piece from time to time. When the chicken is a light brown colour, add the button onions and mushrooms. Cover and cook slowly for 5 minutes. Add the white wine. Season. Cover and simmer until tender. Take off the lid, add the cream. Correct seasoning. Serve hot or cold.

CHICKEN CURRY

(This is a rich and wonderful way of making curry and offers an alternative to the method mentioned on page 184, Rice.)
1 boiling chicken. 1 cooking apple. 1 tablespoon flour. 1 oz. curry powder. ½ lemon. ½ orange. 2 large onions, finely chopped. 1 oz. desiccated coconut. ½ pint cream. 1 pint stock. 1 bay-leaf. 4 cloves of garlic, finely chopped. Seasoning of salt and pepper.

Cut chicken into 8 pieces. (Legs in 2, body in 4). Heat a little margarine in a pan, add chicken and lightly colour, turning the pieces over from time to time. Add onion and cook for a further 10 minutes. Add curry, cook for 2 minutes. Add flour, cook again for 3 or 4 minutes. Stir in stock. Add coconut, lemon, orange, bay-leaf and garlic. Season to taste. Cover and simmer slowly until chicken is tender. When ready, remove lemon and orange. Add 2 dessertspoons cream. Serve with plain boiled rice.
A variety of accompaniments may be served with curry, such as, sliced banana, grated coconut, chopped almonds, and pass round separately puppodums, chutney, etc.

An ever-popular chicken recipe is:—

BOILED CHICKEN AND RICE (with Suprême sauce)

1—5 lb. boiling chicken. 4 oz. rice. 2 oz. butter. 2 onions. 2 carrots. 1 oz. flour. ¼ pint cream. Seasoning of salt and pepper. 1 celery. 1 leek.

Clean the chicken, wash, dry well, place in a pan of cold water. Prepare vegetables and add whole to the pot ; add salt ; bring to the boil, then cover and let simmer slowly for 1 to 2½ hours (according to the quality of the fowl). Prepare Suprême sauce and keep hot. Prepare Rice Pilaff (see page 185). Remove the fowl, skin, cut off the wings, then the breasts, remove the bone, cut the legs in 2. Place a portion of rice pilaff on each plate, top with 1 piece of white meat and 1 piece of leg and cover with hot Suprême sauce.

With any remains of the boiled chicken, the excellent dish of Toast of Chicken Princess Ida (see Turkey, page 88) may be prepared.

GOOSE

In season all the year round but best at Michaelmas. Yellow bills and soft fat feet when young, red when old. Feet should be pliable.

BASIC WAYS OF COOKING

Braise, roast, stew. (Duck recipes are suitable for goose.)

ROAST GOOSE

1 *young goose. Seasoning of salt and pepper.*

Wash well inside, dry at once, season inside and out, and stuff at the tail end with sage and onion or other suitable stuffing. (See Stuffings, pages 181-2). Put pieces of fat bacon or dripping on the breast and roast in medium oven (1 to 2 hours for 9-12 lb., 2½ to 3½ hours for 17-24 lb.) Baste and turn over from time to time ; prick legs occasionally to allow surplus fat to escape. When ready, remove wish-bone with a sharp knife to facilitate carving ; carve in thin slices. Serve with apple sauce and gravy.

If desired, instead of stuffing the tail-end of the goose, this stuffing may be cooked and served separately :—

Finely chop 2 onions ; take a little fat from the roasting-tray, place it in a saucepan, add onions and cook slowly for 10 to 15 minutes ; add 1 teaspoon rubbed sage and a pinch of thyme. Stir well. Mix in 8 oz. white bread-crumbs (soaked bread may be used instead of bread-crumbs), season, add 2 tablespoons gravy and cook in the oven for 15 minutes.

With left-over goose and any left-over lamb :—

CASSOULET À LA TOULOUSAINE

Left-over roast goose, cut into large pieces. Left-over lamb, diced. ¼ lb. pickled pork skin. 2 peeled and chopped onions. Bouquet garni. Speck of garlic. 1 tablespoon flour. 1 cup stock. 1 tablespoon tomato purée. Seasoning of salt and pepper. 1 lb. haricot beans (soaked overnight, cooked for 2 hours before using for the Cassoulet). Garlic sausage, sliced.

Put into a sautipan—lamb, pickled pork skin, bouquet garni, speck of garlic, onions, and fry until brown ; strain off fat ; add flour to ingredients and stir well ; cover with stock and tomato purée. Season and cook slowly for ¾ hour. Place alternately in a casserole dish—1 layer of goose, 1 layer of garlic sausage and 1 layer of haricot beans—finish with layer of beans. Pour sauce mixture into the casserole and cook in the oven for approximately ¾ hour.

With goose neck, heart and liver :—

STUFFED GOOSE NECK

With sharp knife separate goose neck skin from tube which runs through centre of neck ; peel off skin "inside out" and marinate it for

4 hours (or overnight) in ½ measure brandy and seasoning of salt, pepper, pinch of cinnamon and clove. Turn skin "right side out" and stuff with finely chopped goose heart and liver, 1 cup sausage meat, and 1 diced truffle; add marinade and mix very thoroughly. Sew skin of neck at each end, then shallow-fry in goose fat. Serve sliced.

Goose liver may be prepared as follows :—

GOOSE LIVER PIEMONTESE

Flour, toss and fry medallions of goose liver in butter; serve accompanied by risotto and garnished with truffle slices. Note.—The lucullus goose liver should not be overcooked and the middle should remain rosy.

The French luxury speciality of Paté de Foie Gras is made with goose liver. It originates from the Alsace or the "Toulousaine" area, and Alsace livers are considered more firm.

My father—"Mario"—has created a charming savoury with Foie Gras:—

CANAPÉ À LA MARIO

Take a piece of foie gras, mash it with a fork and spread it on a round of hot toast; sprinkle with chopped almonds. Put under the grill or in the oven till brown and serve very hot.

TURKEY

In season all the year round but best at Christmas for which season specially bred and fattened.

When young, legs are smooth and dark; when old, rough and reddish. Best to choose a turkey which is white with legs faintly blue. (Make sure that the whiteness of the bird is not due to flour with which the merchant has covered it.) Eyes should be clear and wattles bright red.

For not more than 8 people, advisable to choose hen turkey 9 to 10 lb. which has very large breast but smaller bone formation so that, although slightly dearer, it renders more edible meat to the lb. ; also fits well into a small oven. Have tendons drawn from the legs when buying.

BASIC WAYS OF COOKING

Braise, roast, stew.

ROAST TURKEY

1 *turkey. Seasoning of salt and pepper. Dripping.*

Clean, wash well the turkey, season, stuff with Chestnut stuffing (see Stuffings, page 179). Remove wish-bone from the turkey before stuffing as this allows slices of turkey and stuffing to be cut straight through. Place bird on its side, resting on the leg, thus juices are not drained from the breast ; cover with dripping and place in a hot oven for 20 minutes ; lower the temperature and continue to roast, turning over from leg to leg and basting occasionally. Test whether it is cooked by feeling the end of the leg ; if the flesh is tender and if the leg comes away easily from the bone, the turkey is cooked. Allow to stand 15 minutes before carving for the birds to set. (Keep hot.) Always leave the turkey to set lying on the breast so that any juice will run through and keep the breast moist. Remove legs before carving.

Serve with cranberry sauce.

Turkey remains may be used, as below :—

MAYONNAISE OF TURKEY

Pieces of cold turkey. Lettuce, finely shredded (or one of the winter salads, i.e., curly endive, batavia, Belgian endive, escarole). 2 hardboiled eggs, sliced. 2 tomatoes, peeled and quartered. Mayonnaise sauce. 6 fillets of anchovies. Capers.

Place turkey pieces on a bed of finely shredded lettuce ; cover with mayonnaise sauce ; decorate edges of the bowl with tomatoes and eggs ; place fillets of anchovies on the mayonnaise and sprinkle with a few capers.

TURKEY PANCAKES

For Pancake Mixture :—

½ lb. flour. 1¼ pints milk. 3 eggs. ¼ teaspoon of salt.

Sift flour, add salt ; beat eggs with 1 pint of milk. Add flour and beat until smooth. Leave for as long as possible, then add remainder of milk.

For Turkey Mixture :—

Turkey pieces, picked from the carcase and legs, very finely chopped. 1 oz. butter. 1 small onion, finely chopped. ½ cup milk. 1 tablespoon cornflour. Seasoning of salt and pepper.

Place butter into a saucepan, add onion and cook without colouring for 5 minutes ; add chopped turkey and mix well ; add milk, boil, thicken with cornflour. Season, cover, and let simmer slowly for 1 hour.
Make thick pancakes, using red-hot frying-pan and minimum amount of fat, and spread a little of the hot turkey mixture on to each pancake before folding. (Use 3 pancakes per portion.) Place in a flat dish, cover with cream and a sprinkling of grated Parmesan cheese, then brown quickly either in a hot oven or under the grill.

TOAST OF TURKEY PRINCESS IDA

Using scalloped pieces of turkey, proceed exactly as for Turkey Mixture (Turkey Pancakes) above.

Place mixture on large rounds of hot buttered toast, top each portion with a freshly poached egg, cover with cream, sprinkle with grated Parmesan cheese, and lightly brown in the oven or under the grill.

With the bones of the turkey make :—

POTAGE

Boil up all the bones, well covered with water; add any left-over vegetables, season, and pass through a sieve.

With the turkey neck, giblets, winglets, plus turkey bones (or a few bones from the butcher) make :—

MINESTRINA OF RICE AND POTATOES

Place the neck, giblets, winglets, plus bones, into a saucepan; cover with cold water, bring to the boil, skim well, add 2 carrots, 2 onions, a few celery stalks; simmer for 2 to 3 hours. Strain. Add 2 large potatoes, peeled and very finely sliced, and cook for 5 minutes; add 1 cup of washed rice and simmer for 15 minutes; add 1 cup grated Parmesan cheese. Mix well. Serve. Pass round a dish of grated Parmesan cheese.

With turkey stock, make :—

ONION SOUP

Simmer bones, covered well with water. Halve and thinly slice 1 or 2 large onions and let simmer slowly in turkey fat or a little butter until golden; pour stock and 1 measure of brandy on to them, correct seasoning.
Pass round separately a dish of grated Parmesan cheese.

DUCK

In season all the year round. Should be soft, white, have supple feet and hard plump breasts.
Tame ducks have yellow feet.
Duckling is a young duck but which can reach as much as 6 lb. in weight. Small duckling is best, I think, roasted, but, of course, large duckling may be cooked in the same way as duck.

BASIC WAYS OF COOKING

Braise, roast, stew.

ROAST DUCK

Clean and stuff duck at the tail end. Prune or sage and onion are popular stuffings (see Stuffings, pages 181—2). Spread fat on top and dust with salt. Roast for 1 hour or according to size. Ducklings—25 to 40 minutes, according to size. Serve with apple sauce.

For that "different" recipe : —

DUCK À L'ANANAS

1 *large duck.* 4 *oz. sliced pineapple, fresh or tinned.* ½ *pint brown sauce.* 1 *teaspoon pineapple jam (or redcurrant jelly).* 1 *measure port or marsala. Seasoning of salt and pepper.*

Clean, wash, dry well, season, and truss the duck. Place in a roasting tray, add a little fat, and roast for 40 to 50 minutes, according to size. Remove the duck. Pour off fat in the tray into a basin ;

heat the sediment until very hot indeed, add port and jam, cook together for 5 minutes ; strain into a saucepan and add brown sauce ; let simmer slowly until required.

Remove breast and wing of duck in one piece and cut in two ; cut each leg in two. Arrange pieces on a hot platter and top with sliced pineapple. Keep hot.

Skim the sauce well, correct seasoning, and pour over the duck.

DUCK À L'ORANGE

1 large duck. 3 oranges. 1 measure of sherry. 1 dessertspoon redcurrant jelly. ⅓ pint brown sauce. Seasoning of salt and pepper.

Clean and season the duck inside and out. Roast in a hot oven for approximately 10 minutes until sealed, then lower to moderate heat and continue roasting for 40 to 50 minutes. Keep hot. Meanwhile, remove the rind from the oranges, cut them into fine strips, place in a saucepan with the sherry and cook for 5 minutes. Remove all white pith from the oranges and the segments ; squeeze the orange juice into the brown sauce ; add redcurrant jelly, sherry and orange rind, season. Strain. Cut the duck, decorate with the segments of orange, and pour over the sauce.

If desired, add 2 tablespoons brandy to the sauce just before pouring over the duck.

And here is a recipe for young duck :—

DUCK À LA ROUENNAISE

1 duckling. 1 measure red wine. 1 tablespoon brandy. ⅓ pint brown sauce. Duck livers. Seasoning of salt and pepper, Cayenne pepper and juice of ¼ lemon.

Roast the duckling and leave underdone. Remove the legs and breast. Skin. Carve into thin slices, place on a dish. Keep warm but *not hot*. Pour off all the fat in the roasting-tray. Heat the sediment, add the red wine, and bring to the boil. Strain into a saucepan, add the brown sauce; re-boil and then let simmer. Finely chop the livers; press the carcase to remove all the blood possible; skim blood to remove every trace of fat; then mix blood and livers together.

Remove sauce from the fire, add blood and livers to it; mix quickly with a whisk until it thickens slightly. DO NOT RE-BOIL. Season. Add brandy. Pour sauce over the fillets.

With left-overs, the following handy dish may be made:—

CASSEROLE (Duck or any poultry or meat remnants may be used)

Duck left-overs, cut into pieces but not boned. 2 shallots, finely chopped. 1 piece of crushed garlic. ¼ lb. mushrooms, peeled and sliced. 2 tomatoes, peeled and sliced. 1 cup stock or 1 measure white wine or sherry. 1 sprig marjoram. 1 teaspoon chopped parsley. Seasoning of salt and pepper.

Fill well buttered casserole dish with shallots, tomatoes, mushrooms, garlic, marjoram, duck remnants, and season. Pour in stock or wine and bake in moderate oven for 20 minutes. Garnish with chopped parsley before serving. If desired, ¾ cup cream may be added with the stock.

With the carcase, giblets, etc., make a duck stock which may be used for the following fabulous soup:—

BORTSCH À LA RUSSE (It must be borne in mind that a duck stock is essential in this

recipe, so this soup should be subsequent to a meal of roast duck)

2 *pints duck stock.* ¼ *of white cabbage.* 1 *raw beetroot* (½ *for soup,* ½ *for beetroot vinegar*). ⅛ *pint vinegar.* 1 *carrot.* 1 *turnip.* ¼ *of red cabbage.* 1 *leek.* ⅛ *pint cream* (*sour preferable*). *Seasoning of salt and pepper.*

Finely shred all the vegetables. Bring stock to the boil. Add the vegetables and cook for 10 to 15 minutes. Season to taste, and add a little finely-shredded duck meat. (This can be taken from the carcase before stock is made.) Serve very hot.

Grate the remaining beetroot, add to the vinegar, stand for 30 minutes, strain. Serve the beetroot vinegar and sour cream in separate sauceboats. A few small meat patties served hot accompany the soup very well.

With liver:—

MOCK PÂTÉ DE FOIE GRAS (Use as a Canapé spread)

Cooked duck (*or any poultry*) *livers. Seasoning of salt, pepper and lemon juice.*

Mash livers and season.
Better results can be obtained if the livers are passed through a fine sieve.

PIGEON

In season all the year round. Should be plump. When young, have supple feet.
Tame pigeons are larger than wild pigeons but not as large as wood-pigeons.
Allow 1 pigeon per person.

Bake, braise, broil, roast, stew, sauté.

ROAST PIGEON

Clean and truss pigeons, put in roasting-tray, cover breasts with bacon or fat ; cook in the oven for 20 to 30 minutes. Serve with bread sauce.

WOOD-PIGEON IN ALE

Livers of pigeon. Veal stuffing (see page 182). 1 pint water. Bouquet garni. ½ pint mild ale. 2 small peeled and chopped onions.

Stuff the pigeons with livers and veal stuffing mixed well together ; place in stew-pan, cover with ale and water, add onion and bouquet garni. Stew for approximately 2 hours. Strain the sauce and pour it over the pigeons. Serve immediately.

With any left-over pieces :—

PIGEON PIE (this recipe is also suitable for rabbit)

Left-over pigeon pieces. Flaky pastry. ¼ pint stock. Seasoning of salt and pepper. 2 shallots, finely chopped.

Put in a pie-dish pigeon pieces, season and sprinkle with chopped shallots ; add stock ; cover with a layer of flaky pastry, seal edges tightly and slit on the top. Bake in a moderate oven for ¾ hour.
If whole pigeons used instead of left-overs, they should be quartered and baked for 1½ hours.

HARE

In season September to end of February, when in plentiful supply. Young hare has smooth sharp claws, ears that tear easily and a narrow cleft in the lip.

Boil, bake, fry, roast, stew.

ROAST HARE À L'ANGLAISE

Wipe hare inside and out. Boil liver, chop and use for stuffing. Stuff hare (Liver Stuffing, see page 181), sew the opening, truss by drawing hind legs forward and front legs backwards under the hare and secure with string or skewers, and cover back with fat bacon. Roast for 1½ to 2 hours. Serve with redcurrant jelly and bread sauce.

JUGGED HARE

2 hares. ½ bottle red wine. 1 measure of port. 1 onion, peeled and sliced. 1 carrot, sliced. 1 bouquet garni with extra thyme. Garlic. 1 teaspoon cornflour. Redcurrant jelly.

Cut open the stomach of each hare, retain in a basin the blood, heart, lungs and liver; discard the rest. Dissect each hare by cutting the legs in 2, the shoulders in 2, and use the back for Rable de Lièvre à la Crême. Place the meat in a basin, cover with red wine, onion, carrot, bouquet garni with plenty of thyme, and leave for at least 24 hours or, if possible, for 1 week. When ready to cook, drain, retain the wine, shallow-fry the hare and vegetables. Place in a saucepan, add wine and plenty of chopped garlic. Season, add a little stock if required. Cover and cook slowly for 2½ to 3 hours. Remove the meat and place on a hot platter. Re-boil the stock, skim well, thicken very lightly with diluted cornflour, cook for 5 minutes.

Finely chop the hearts, livers, etc., and mix with the blood. Remove the sauce from the fire, add the blood, stir well, do not re-boil; add port and 1 tablespoon redcurrant jelly; strain over the hares.

With the backs or saddles :—

RABLE DE LIÈVRE À LA CRÊME (a delicate dish much appreciated by gourmets)

2 hares (use only the saddles skinned with a sharp knife). Red wine. ¼ pint cream. Seasoning of salt and pepper.

Cover the saddles in red wine for 48 hours before using. Drain. Season. Place in a hot roast-pan and roast in a hot oven for 10 to 12 minutes. Leave underdone. Remove. Drain off the surplus fat ; add cream ; season and simmer slowly. Put the 2 saddles on a hot platter, cover with the sauce.

When serving each portion, do not carve the meat because the 2 fillets on each saddle are scooped out easily with a tablespoon. Serve with redcurrant jelly.

HARE SOUP

1 hare. 1 gallon of water. 2 tablespoons fat. ½ cup oatmeal. 2 onions, peeled and sliced. 2 carrots, diced. 2 turnips, diced. 2 parsnips, diced. 2 sticks celery, diced. 6 peppercorns. 2 bay-leaves. ½ teaspoon herbs. 1 measure of sherry.

Skin and clean the hare, and retain the blood carefully ; rinse hare, then cut into pieces, dry, and put in a pan with the fat. Fry with sliced onion until golden, add water, blood and oatmeal, cook slowly until boiling (stirring continually), add vegetables, bay-leaves, peppercorns and herbs, and let simmer for approximately 4 hours. Remove meat, strain liquor and return to pan with hare chopped into small dice. Add sherry and reheat.

RABBIT

In season all the year round. Tame rabbit best. Wild rabbit, although cheaper, not such good value nor flavour.
You can recognize an old rabbit by its thick haunches, dry ears and blunt and ragged claws ; whereas, young rabbit has soft ears and paws, and smooth claws.

BASIC WAYS OF COOKING

Bake, boil, fry, roast, stew, sauté. (Most chicken recipes are suitable for rabbit. Old rabbits more suitable for pies, casseroles.)

BOILED RABBIT À L'ANGLAISE

Clean and wipe rabbit inside and out, boil liver and use for stuffing (see Liver Stuffing, page 181), stuff, sew the opening, truss. Cover well with salted water and cook for approximately 1 hour. Serve with a thick white sauce.

ROAST RABBIT

Clean and wipe rabbit inside and out, stuff, sew the opening, truss, and cover back with fat bacon. Roast for approximately 1 hour.
Serve with Béchamel sauce with added boiled and mashed rabbit liver.

Left-overs may be used as follows :—

RABBIT CHASSEUR

Left-over rabbit pieces. Flour. 3 chopped shallots. ½ cup white wine. 1 cup water. Seasoning of salt and pepper. Bouquet garni. 1 dessertspoon tomato purée. 8 oz. mushrooms, peeled and finely chopped. Chopped parsley.

Flour rabbit pieces, toss and fry in a saucepan ; add shallots, then white wine and water. Add seasoning, bouquet garni and tomato purée. Cook for ¾ hour on a moderate fire, then add mushrooms.
Garnish with chopped parsley before serving.

VENISON

In season all the year round but doe venison best in January, October, November, December, and buck venison best in June, July, August, September.
Should have clear bright fat of considerable thickness. Hang two weeks at least before using.

BASIC WAYS OF COOKING

Fry, grill, roast, stew.

VENISON STEAK

1½ lb. venison steak (Scotch preferable).

Make sure it has been well hung. Grill quickly. Medium-cooked or underdone, never well done. If desired, season with 3 tablespoons madeira wine. Serve with Béarnaise sauce.

SADDLE OF VENISON METTERNICH

Saddle of venison.

Garnish with fine lardoons of fat bacon and marinate. Roast (13 to 15 minutes to the lb. and 15 minutes over). Garnish with braised red cabbages and braised chestnuts, and serve with redcurrant jelly.

MARINADE (used to tenderize the flesh of venison, also game generally)

Put meat in a basin; add a few carrots, slices of shallots and onions, ¼ teaspoon crushed pepper grains, 1 clove, sprig of parsley, sprig of thyme, bay-leaf. Season with salt and cover all with white wine (say, 1 bottle of white wine) and 1 measure vinegar; sprinkle with 2 tablespoons oil. Keep in a cool place and let marinate 24 hours for small meat and 2 to 4 days for large meat.

With left-overs :—

VENISON MILANAISE

Left-over venison, cut into fine slices. 1 truffle, sliced. Smoked tongue. 1 cup macaroni. Tomato purée.

Add truffle and smoked tongue to venison and mix with macaroni and tomato purée. Stew. Serve hot in a hollow dish and sprinkle with grated Parmesan cheese.

GROUSE

In season August 12th to December 10th.
When grouse-shooting is at its height (August 19th to 1st week September) many people are away on holiday in the town areas where, during that period, supply exceeds demand and the prices generally fall ; from an economy point of view, therefore, this is the best time for purchase, for thereafter prices rise again.
Should be plump, have soft feet and pliable bill. A good method of ensuring that a grouse is young is to examine each first wing-feather ; it should have a tiny white dot at the tip of the first feather.

BASIC WAYS OF COOKING

Bake, boil, broil, braise, roast, sauté, stew. (Young grouse better broiled.)

ROAST GROUSE SUR CANAPÉ

4 plump young grouse (1 grouse per portion). 4 slices of bacon. Watercress. 1 dash lemon juice. 4 pieces of shaped bread. Game chips (hot potato crisps). Seasoning of salt and pepper.

Cover each bird with a slice of bacon, season inside and out. Heat a roast-pan with a little fat, place in the grouse. Roast in a hot oven, basting from time to time and turning over every 5 minutes, for 15 to 20 minutes. Remove. Take out the hearts and livers ; mash well with a fork, season and add lemon juice. Fry the pieces of bread in the fat from the roasting-pan, then spread them with the liver-paste. Place a grouse on each piece of bread and garnish each portion with game chips and watercress.

Serve separately—thin gravy, browned bread-crumbs, and bread sauce.

BROILED GROUSE

1 young grouse (per portion). Seasoning of salt and pepper. 2 tablespoons olive oil. 1 large piece of buttered toast (per portion). Maître d'Hôtel butter.

Split grouse down the back but do not separate the halves ; place in a dish and season. Coat with oil and grill quickly each side for 5 to 10 minutes. Serve on toast with Maître d'Hôtel butter spread on it.

GROUSE À LA CRÈME

1 young grouse per portion.
4 young grouse. 4 dabs of butter. 4 slices of bacon. 1 oz. butter. ¼ pint cream. Seasoning of salt and pepper.

Cover the breast of each bird with a slice of bacon, season, and place a dab of butter inside. Roast in a hot oven for 15 to 20 minutes. Remove. Drain off the fat, add cream to the roasting-pan, reduce by slow simmering to half ; remove, season, add 1 oz. butter.

Pour sauce over the grouse.

GROUSE PIE

3 grouses (with removed carcases) cut into 4 pieces. Fine slices of raw beef. Seasoning of salt, pepper, 2 chopped shallots, 2 finely sliced mushrooms, and chopped parsley. 3 hard-boiled egg yolks, cut into pieces. Slices of bacon. 1 cup stock. Flaky pastry.

Layer bottom of pie-dish with beef slices, add grouse pieces, and season. Add egg yolks; put bacon slices between grouse pieces, pour in stock and cover with flaky pastry sealed well at edges and slit on the top. Bake in a moderate oven for 1 hour.

If desired, left-over game pieces and cooked slices of beef may be used for this pie; in which case, bake for 30 to 45 minutes.

PARTRIDGE

In season September 1st to February 1st.
Should have soft feet and pliable bill. Perdreau is a young partridge and has dark-coloured bill. Perdrix is an old partridge. There are 2 types of partridges, however. The grey leg and the red leg. The Frenchman is of the opinion that there is "nothing to touch the red leg," while the Englishman considers the grey leg to be the "one and only partridge." So you can take your choice, for both are available, with the red leg bigger and cheaper.

BASIC WAYS OF COOKING

Bake, braise, broil, roast, stew, sauté. (Young partridge best roasted, old partridge stewed and casseroled.)

ROAST PARTRIDGE AND BACON

4 young partridges (one per portion). 4 slices of bacon. 4 dabs of butter. 4 pieces of shaped bread. ¼ pint stock. Watercress. Game chips (hot potato crisps). Seasoning of salt and pepper.

Cover the breast of each bird with a slice of bacon, season, and place a dab of butter inside.

101

Roast in a hot oven for 15 minutes, basting occasionally. When cooked, remove liver inside, mash with a fork, season, and spread on the fried bread. Place birds on the fried shaped pieces of bread. For gravy :—pour the fat away slowly from the roasting-pan or tray ; retain the juices ; place on full fire, cook until the juices are completely reduced, then add stock. Season, simmer slowly until it has reduced by half. Strain. Garnish each portion with game chips and watercress. Serve separately—gravy, browned breadcrumbs, and bread sauce.

SAUTÉ OF YOUNG PARTRIDGE ELIZABETH

1 young partridge (per portion), cut into 4 pieces. Flour. 1 measure of brandy. ¼ cup thick cream. 1 cup stock. Seasoning of salt and pepper. 1 dessertspoon muscat grapes, peeled and seeded.

Season the partridge pieces, flour and toss in butter in a saucepan. Set alight with brandy ; add stock ; correct seasoning ; cover and cook for 20 minutes. Then add grapes and cream and cook for a further 5 minutes.

PHEASANT

In season October 1st to February 1st. Best at the beginning of the season when young and juicy ; later in the season tend to become dry. Should have soft feet and pliable bill. Spurs of old birds long, hard, and pointed ; spurs of young birds short and round.

Choose a cock pheasant with small spurs. There is no satisfactory method of testing hen pheasants.

Bake, boil, broil, braise, roast, stew, sauté.

ROAST PHEASANT

2 pheasants. 2 slices of fat bacon. 2 dabs of butter·
4 pieces of shaped bread. Game chips (hot potato
crisps). Watercress. Seasoning of salt and pepper.

Cover the breast of each bird with a slice of
bacon, season and place a dab of butter inside.
Roast in the oven for approximately 45 minutes,
basting occasionally. Remove. Serve on fried
bread, garnish with game chips and watercress.
Serve separately—gravy, browned bread-crumbs,
and bread sauce.

It is not widely known that pheasant is delicious boiled : —

BOILED PHEASANT

1 pheasant. 3 sticks celery.

Cover well pheasant and celery with salted water ;
boil for 50 minutes. Drain.
Serve with celery and Velouté sauce. (Use
pheasant stock in the sauce.)

Suitable for an old pheasant (also old partridge) : —

PHEASANT AUX CHOUX

1 large pheasant. 2 carrots. 1 onion, peeled. 1 large
white cabbage. 1 small piece of bacon. 4 Frank-
furter sausages. Seasoning of salt and pepper.

Season pheasant. Place in a pan and roast in
the oven for 30 minutes. Cut the cabbage in 4,
wash well, place in boiling water and boil for 5
minutes. Remove. Place the cabbage in a deep
pan, add the pheasant with fat and juice
from the pan, carrots, onion and bacon. Cover

tightly and cook in oven for 1 to 1½ hours. Put in the Frankfurter sausages during the last 5 minutes. Cut the pheasant, slice the bacon and carrots. To serve, place a portion of cabbage on each plate, 1 piece of pheasant, 1 slice of bacon, 1 sausage, and decorate with sliced carrots ; add a little of the stock around the plate.

As choicest parts of pheasant are the breast and the wings :—

BREAST OF PHEASANT PÉRIGOURDINE

2 young pheasants. Slices of fat bacon. 2 slices of foie gras, lighty sautéed in butter for 1 minute. 2 slices of truffle.

Clean pheasants and truss so as to hold legs and wings close to bodies, tie slice of bacon on to breasts. Put birds on their sides in a roasting-tray and roast each side in a hot oven for ½ hour. Carve the birds and place breasts on a hot platter. Garnish breasts with slice of foie gras and truffle. Serve with madeira sauce.

WOODCOCK

During latter part of winter, nature adds a layer of fat which renders meat tender and succulent. When young, feet are soft and tender.

BASIC WAYS OF COOKING

Bake, roast.

ROAST WOODCOCK

1 woodcock (per portion). Livers of woodcock. 1 piece of toast. Seasoning of salt and pepper.

Cover woodcock with dripping or bacon and roast in very hot oven for 12 to 15 minutes ; should be served underdone. Finely chop livers,

season, spread on buttered toast, place in hot
oven for 1 or 2 minutes.
Serve woodcock whole on toast.

WOODCOCK AU CHAMPAGNE

*Woodcock, cut into pieces. Crushed intestines.
1 tablespoon butter. 1 measure champagne, dry
or half-dry. Seasoning of salt and pepper.*

Toss woodcock pieces and fry quickly in hot
butter; season. Put pieces into a casserole dish
with champagne, add crushed intestines, and
bake for 15 to 20 minutes.

PLOVER, SNIPE, TEAL, WIDGEON

During latter part of winter, nature adds a layer of fat which
renders meat tender and succulent. When young, feet are soft
and tender. Golden plover is best in December.

May be cooked in similar manner as woodcock.

QUAIL

A very delicate and succulent bird. Quail has become rare here;
most supplies used to come from Egypt.

BASIC WAYS OF COOKING

Bake, roast.

ROAST QUAIL (May be cooked with or without vine-leaves, but vine-leaves, if available,
do improve the flavour)

*Quails (1 or 2 per portion). Slices of bacon.
Vine-leaves. Seasoning of salt and pepper.*

Clean and truss quails; wrap each in a slice of
bacon, then into a vine-leaf. Season. Place in

a roasting-tray and cook in a very hot oven for 7 to 10 minutes. Serve with gravy.

QUAIL VERONIQUE

Quails (1 or 2 per portion). Slices of bacon. Seasoning of salt and pepper. 1 oz. butter. 1 tablespoon brandy. 1 tablespoon peeled and seeded muscat grapes.

Clean and truss quails; wrap each in a slice of bacon. Place close together in a small saucepan, season, add butter. Start cooking on top of the stove; when hot cover and leave in a hot oven for 7 to 8 minutes. Take out of the oven and remove bacon and fat. Replace quails into the saucepan, add brandy and grapes. Cook slowly for 5 minutes. Place quails on a hot dish and cover with grapes and remaining liqueur before serving. If desired, grapes may be omitted from this recipe and the quails may be served with the liqueur and risotto.

WILD DUCK

During latter part of winter, nature adds a layer of fat which renders meat tender and succulent. Wild duck have red feet.

BASIC WAYS OF COOKING

Bake, braise, broil, roast, stew, sauté.

ROAST WILD DUCK

Clean wild duck, truss and put in roasting-tray with a piece of fat bacon or fat on the breast. Roast in hot oven for 15 minutes. Serve with redcurrant jelly.

WILD DUCK AU PORTO

2 large wild ducks. 1 teaspoon cornflour. Juice of ½ lemon. 1 large glass of port. 1 dessertspoon redcurrant jelly. Seasoning of salt, pepper and cayenne pepper.

Season ducks inside and out. Roast in hot oven for approximately 10 minutes ; leave very underdone. Remove the legs and cook them for a further 10 minutes. Meanwhile, remove the wishbone of each duck with a sharp knife, making it easier to take off the two breasts which are skinned and carved into fine fillets. When the legs are ready, place them on a dish covered with a display of fillets. Keep in hot-plate.

For the sauce :—Chop the carcases very fine and press hard through a fine strainer to extract as much blood as possible. Strain the fat carefully from the roasting-tray, retaining the sediment ; place in pan on full fire, add port, redcurrant jelly, lemon juice, bring to the boil, thicken with diluted cornflour, cook slowly for 10 minutes. Strain, add blood, season.

Pour sauce over the fillets.

When the blood has been extracted from the carcase, carefully remove any traces of fat before adding to the sauce.

Any left-over game pieces may be used for a :—

SALMI (also suitable for duck pieces left-over)

Slowly reheat pieces in Spanish sauce. Do not let boil or meat will harden.

FISH, SHELLFISH, MOLLUSCS

Nowadays it is customary for a fishmonger to skin, fillet, or carry out any preparations desired to fish purchased. (Use fish-slice for carving fish and not a steel knife.)

THERE ARE THREE MAIN CLASSES OF FISH:—

1. *Oily, containing fatty oil dispersed throughout the flesh; excellent food value (i.e., salmon, herring, mackerel, pilchard).*
2. *White or non-oily (lean), containing fat secreted in the liver, which is removed in cleaning process (i.e., hake, cod, turbot, whiting, halibut, sole, haddock, and all flat fish).*
3. *Shellfish, such as lobsters, crab, crayfish, shrimps and prawns, and molluscs like mussels and oysters. Not considered of high food value, excepting oysters.*

TO SELECT FISH:—

Make sure it is fresh. Flesh should be firm and there is more value to a thick-through fish. Odour pleasant, and not akin to ammonia. Scales plentiful; a little slime on the skin in addition to being shiny. Fins stiff. Eyes very bright. Gills, when visible, fresh pink or red. Fish from deeper waters possess skins of darker hue for protective purposes.

And fresh fish sinks in water!

BASS

(Fresh-water.) A game fish, greenish with darker markings.
Weight, 4 lb. upwards. Firm white flesh.

BASIC WAYS OF COOKING

May be cooked whole, boiled and served hot or cold, or baked
with butter and herbs. Filleted bass is tasty grilled, or cooked
and served in a sauce.

BREAM

(Fresh-water or sea fish.) Silvery-pink with rich firm flesh, oily.
Weight, 2 to 3 lb.

BASIC WAYS OF COOKING

Sea bream for recipes given for mackerel or red mullet; excellent grilled and sprinkle well with lemon juice and chopped
herbs before serving; it may be filleted or cooked whole.
Fresh-water bream must be thoroughly washed and soaked in
a little salt water before cooking. Stuff with a savoury stuffing
and serve with a piquant sauce.

BRILL

(Sea-fish.) In season all the year round. A fine fish. Cut fish
should be firm and close-grained and not blue.

BASIC WAYS OF COOKING

May be cooked in similar ways as turbot, served whole or in
fillets.

CARP

(Fresh-water.) In season mid-June to mid-March. The head
of carp is considered a delicacy. It is interesting to note that
caviare from Sweden, Norway and Denmark is nearly always
carp eggs.

BASIC WAYS OF COOKING

Fry, steam, boil.

CODLING

(Sea fish.) In season all the year round. This small type of cod has a flesh more delicate than that of cod.

BASIC OF WAYS COOKING

May be served whole, bake, grill, hot or cold with a garnish.

COD

(Sea fish.) In season all the year round. Back and sides greenish with brown spots. Cut fish should be firm and close-grained and not blue. Thick part of back is considered best ; it should be carved in unbroken slices, and each solid slice should be accompanied by a bit of the sound, from under back-bone, or from cheek, tongue, jaws, etc., of the head. The liver and roes of cod are considered delicacies.

BASIC WAYS OF COOKING

Bake, boil, grill. Cod roes (hard roes)—dipped in batter and fried in deep fat.

DAB

Small flat-fish or flounder. In season all the year round.

BASIC WAYS OF COOKING

Fry, boil, steam.

EELS

(Fresh-water or sea-water.) In season all the year round. Black or grey-black with greasy gelatinous flesh. Must be freshly killed and skinned immediately. Usually cut into several pieces, either for stew or fry, and thick parts are considered the best.

LAMPREY (fresh-water). Resembles eel and is similarly treated and cooked. Eating too many of these is said to have killed poor King Henry I of England !

BASIC WAYS OF COOKING

Boil, broil, fry, bake, stew. (Clean and wash immediately.)

BOILED EELS

Boil in Court Bouillon (see "Court Bouillon"—
Savoury Sauces, page 159) ; or—plain boil and
serve with caper sauce.

SMOKED EEL

Cut into 3-inch sections, garnish with quartered
lettuce and quartered tomato. Pass round horse-
radish sauce separately.

STEWED EELS

Cut eels into pieces, place in a pan with enough
water to cover and simmer for 20 minutes. Strain,
and add them to white sauce or parsley sauce.
Put into a casserole and cook in the oven for
1 hour.

FRIED EELS

Cut eels into pieces 3 inches long, egg and bread-
crumb, then fry in deep hot fat for 5 minutes ;
drain. Serve with Vinaigrette sauce.

EELS MATELOTE

Cut eels into "finger" type sections ; layer bottom
of a casserole dish with onion slices and shallot
slices, speck of garlic, mixed herbs, seasoning of
salt and grains of pepper ; add eel pieces ; add 1
measure of brandy and moisten with red wine.
Cook for 20 minutes. Remove eel to a hot platter.
Meanwhile, reduce the liquor and mix with 2 oz.
butter and flour to make a light creamy sauce.
Pour this sauce over the eels, and garnish with
cooked mushrooms and small glazed onions.

JELLIED EELS

Cut eels into sections, cover with cold water,
season, bring to the boil. Simmer for 10 minutes.
Pour into a basin. Allow to set. Serve *iced*.

HADDOCK

Similar to cod with smaller mouth and dark spot behind head. Rigidity of flesh, redness of gills, and brightness of eyes denotes freshness. Keeps on ice longer than most varieties.

Finnan haddie is none other than Finland haddock, or—to put it more plainly—smoked haddock !

BASIC WAYS OF COOKING

Bake, boil, grill, steam.

BAKED FINNAN HADDIE

Finnan haddie. Milk and water. Butter.

Put fish in greased pan, cover with milk and water in equal proportions, and let stand over low heat or in slow oven for 25 minutes. Then pour off liquid, spread with butter, and bake for 20 minutes in a moderate oven.

If desired, after letting stand over low heat for 25 minutes, arrange fish in oven-proof dish, pour over white sauce, and surround with peeled and halved potatoes. Then bake in a moderate oven for 30 to 40 minutes.

HADDOCK WITH MILK

1 *lb. haddock.* ½ *tablespoon finely chopped shallot.* 1 *tablespoon finely chopped green pepper.* ½ *tablespoon finely chopped red pepper.* ¼ *cup butter. Seasoning of salt, paprika and cayenne pepper. 4 tablespoons flour. 1 cup cream. 1 cup milk.*

Soak haddock in milk 1 hour ; bake in moderate oven for 30 minutes. Cook shallots and peppers in butter for 5 minutes, stirring continually. Add seasoning, and stir until blended ; then pour on gradually milk and cream. Bring to boiling point and add haddock. Serve on squares of toast or turn into buttered baking dish, cover with bread-crumbs and bake until browned.

HADDOCK MONTE CARLO

Haddock. Milk. 1 large tomato, cut in 2, pips removed. Seasoning of salt and pepper. 1 tablespoon cream. Knob of butter. Poached egg.

Cook haddock in milk. Remove haddock-bone ; then place fish on a dish. Cut tomato halves, season, and place in a heap on the haddock ; bake in the oven for 10 minutes. Reduce milk to one-third, stir in cream and butter. Top haddock with poached egg ; pour over the sauce and brown quickly under the grill. Serve at once.

HAKE

(Sea-water.) In season all the year round. Non-oily cut fish and should be firm and close-grained and not blue.

BASIC WAYS OF COOKING

Boil, broil, bake, fry. Best way to dress hake is to cut it transversely to the length into slices about 1 inch in thickness, fry and garnish with chopped parsley.

HALIBUT

(Sea-fish.) In season all the year except the month of August. A flat-fish with both eyes on right side ; dark above and whitish below.
Cut fish should be firm and close-grained and not blue. Good food value. Tit-bits are the pickings from the head and the flackers over the fins.

BASIC WAYS OF COOKING

Bake, boil, steam, fry, braise. May be cooked in similar ways as turbot.

HERRING

In season in winter. Most important food fish. Silvery and firm thin scales, plump preferable. If neither smoked (kippers or bloaters) nor salted herrings, should be eaten very fresh.

Bake, grill, souse. (May be smoked, salted, split, dried, or pickled).

Herring roes (soft roes) are served on toast as a savoury.

The following is a popular English breakfast dish :—

KIPPERS (Smoked Herrings)

Take required number of kippers, soak for 10 minutes, cut off heads and tails, sprinkle with pepper, put small piece of fat on each and place in greased baking tin. Cover with greased paper and bake in a moderate oven for 15 minutes.

GRILLED KIPPERS

Grill in butter and serve with hot melted butter.

GRILLED HERRINGS

Grill herrings (herrings split and boned and then grilled definitely better than grilled whole) and serve with mustard sauce (Hollandaise sauce with addition of 1 teaspoon English mustard).

MACKEREL

In season in winter. Rich, oily, fatty fish with dark red gills, a very bright eye, a bluish and greenish and silver iridescence but tends to darken quickly ; if gills are not red, it is stale. Roes of mackerel are considered a delicacy.

BASIC WAYS OF COOKING

Grill (split), souse, boil (never divide through when boiled), broil (split). When a large mackerel—should be served in pieces cut through the side. When a small mackerel—may be divided through backbone and served in halves. Shoulder considered best part.

GRILLED MACKEREL

Split mackerel, grill, and serve with Maître d'Hôtel butter on top.

SOUSED MACKEREL

See Basic Methods of Cooking Fish, page 156.

GREY MULLET

(Sea-fish.) In season all the year round. Greenish silvery colour.

BASIC WAYS OF COOKING

May be cooked in similar manner as red mullet but not considered as fine a dish.

RED MULLET

(Sea-fish.) Game of the sea. In season all the year round and what a delectable dish ! Highly esteemed food fish of bright red colour. If too large a fish for one person, divide into two parts ; the liver is a great delicacy and there is delicious picking in the head and brain.

BASIC WAYS OF COOKING

Sauté (dust with flour and sauté in butter).

ROUGET BORDELAISE

4 red mullets (1 per portion). 2 oz. chopped shallots. ½ bottle red wine. 2 oz. butter. Seasoning of salt, pepper and cayenne pepper.

Grease a pan, place in the fish, sprinkle with shallots, season. Add wine. Cover with greaseproof paper and cook in the oven. When ready, remove the fish, reduce the stock by two-thirds. Take away from the fire, work in the butter, correct the seasoning, then pour the sauce over the fish.

ROUGET MEUNIÈRE

Red mullets.

Dip fish in milk and roll in flour ; put in a pan of boiling butter, season with salt, sauté until browned lightly. Serve on a hot platter, pour the sauce over, sprinkle with lemon juice, and garnish with slices of lemon and chopped parsley.

PERCH

(Fresh-water fish.) In season after 15th June to end of March. Varies in colour from yellow, greyish green to blue, with dark brown stripes. Should be firm with clear fresh eyes. Flesh sweet and appetizing.

BASIC WAYS OF COOKING

Boil, bake, fry, grill, steam. If small, serve whole. If large, may be divided through the backbone and served in halves.

PLAICE

In season from May to end of January.
A flat-fish which makes very good eating. Dark-skinned side of plaice, the spots should be bright red and not brown, for brown suggests a tendency toward "old age." Should be firm and not limp.

BASIC WAYS OF COOKING

Bake, fry, grill, poach, sauté.

FRIED PLAICE

Dust filleted plaice with flour, dip in beaten egg, blanket evenly with bread-crumbs, fry one side for 2 minutes, turn and fry other side for about 2 minutes.

PLAICE MEUNIÈRE

Dip filleted plaice in milk and roll in flour ; put in a pan of boiling butter, season with salt, sauté until browned lightly. Serve on a hot platter, pour the sauce over, sprinkle with lemon juice, and garnish with slices of lemon and chopped parsley.

ROCK SALMON

(Sea-water fish.) (Fishmonger's name for large sea-blenny.) In season all the year round. Popular and reasonable.

BASIC WAYS OF COOKING

Fry, boil, stew.

SALMON

(The king of fresh-water fish.) In season 1st February to mid-August ; inclined to be coarse during height of summer. (Scottish best ; Irish also very good.)

Brownish above with silvery sides black dotted ; firm pink or reddish-orange flesh. When perfectly fresh, there is a creamy substance between flakes.

"Red caviare" is spawn of salmon.

SALMON TROUT. All salmon recipes are suitable for salmon trout.

SMOKED SALMON. In season all the year round but best in summer.

BASIC WAYS OF COOKING

Poach, boil, bake, fry, grill, braise, steam. Serve cold or hot.

SMOKED SALMON MOSCOVITE

8 slices of smoked salmon. 4 oz. caviare. 2 lemons.

Roll the salmon slices in cornet shapes ; stuff each with caviare. Serve very cold with ½ lemon per portion. Accompany with finely sliced brown bread and butter.

SALMON AND CUCUMBER

1 slice of salmon per person. 1 onion, peeled and sliced. 1 carrot, scraped, and sliced. 1 cucumber. 1 tablespoon vinegar. 2 hard-boiled eggs. 2 tomatoes. Seasoning of salt and pepper.

Wipe salmon, put in pan, cover with cold water, add vinegar, onion, carrot, seasoning. Bring to the boil. Remove. Cool in the stock. When cold, remove skin and bone. Garnish each portion with finely-sliced cucumber, quartered eggs and tomatoes. Serve with mayonnaise or hollandaise sauce. (May be served hot or cold.)

GRILLED SALMON

Season salmon cutlets with salt, place dabs of butter on each, grill each side thoroughly, regularly basting with the melted butter. Garnish with slices of lemon and chopped parsley. Serve with mayonnaise or hollandaise sauce.

With left-overs which are around the head and the tail make "Coquille of Fish" or "Salmon Mayonnaise" (see Remnants, pages 146, 153). Salmon trout left-overs may be used in the same way.

COLD SALMON TROUT

1 salmon trout. 1 onion, peeled and sliced. 1 carrot, scraped and sliced. 1 cucumber. 1 tablespoon vinegar. 2 hard-boiled eggs. 2 tomatoes. Seasoning of salt and pepper.

Wipe salmon trout, put in pan, cover with cold water, add vinegar, onion, carrot, seasoning. Bring to the boil. Remove. Cool in the stock. When cold, remove the trout, take off the skin, leave the head intact, and place on a serving-dish. Garnish the length of the fish with finely-sliced cucumber, and surround with quartered eggs and tomatoes. Serve with Verte sauce.

SALMON TROUT DORIA

Grilled in butter, garnish with cooked and shaped cucumbers.

SALMON TROUT CHAMPAGNE

1 salmon trout (2½ lb. to 3 lb.). ¼ bottle champagne or dry white wine. ¼ pint cream. 2 oz. butter. ½ oz. flour. 1 chopped shallot. Seasoning of salt and pepper, cayenne pepper and lemon juice.

Place salmon trout in a buttered dish, add shallots, champagne, seasoning; cover with greaseproof paper; bring to the boil. Then cook in the oven for 15 minutes. Remove. Drain stock into a saucepan, and reduce. Skin the trout, leave the head intact, place on a dish. (Keep warm.) Mix together flour and ½ oz. butter, add this to stock, whisk well until smooth; add cream. Remove from fire and work in remainder of butter, add dash of cayenne pepper and a few drops lemon juice. Strain over fish.

SKATE

In season in winter. A popular and reasonable flat-fish.

BASIC WAYS OF COOKING

Fry (very nice fried in egg and bread-crumbs), boil.

SKATE AU BEURRE NOIR

Boil the skate, clean, and place on a hot platter (keep hot). Meanwhile, prepare the Beurre Noir (black butter). Season the skate with salt and pepper, garnish with capers and chopped parsley. Then pour the Beurre Noir on the fish. Add 2 tablespoons vinegar to butter remaining in pan, stir until reduced to half, and pour straight away on the fish. Serve very hot.

SMELTS

In season October to June. (Found in tidal waters.) Related to salmon but small and silvery. Delicate flavour.

BASIC WAYS OF COOKING

Fry, grill.

FRIED ÉPERLANS (smelts)

12 *smelts (serves* 4 *persons).*

Clean smelts and remove fins. Bread-crumb, fry in deep fat, drain, season. Serve with Tartare sauce and fried parsley.

SMELTS À L'ANGLAISE

Slowly grill in butter and serve with melted butter.

SOLE

Dover sole (sea-water). Lemon sole (lean and non-oily). In season all the year round.

DOVER SOLE—rather long opposed to being wide. Considered a "sacrilege" to have head taken off this delicious flat-fish, so *never* ask your fishmonger to break this golden rule!

LEMON SOLE—smaller and wider than the ordinary sole; light brown in colour and dotted with small spots; it is used more for filleting than Dover sole.

BASIC WAYS OF COOKING

Fry, grill, poach. (When served whole, black skin removed and white skin scaled, and should be sliced across before cooking.)

FILLET OF SOLE BONNE FEMME

2 large soles. 1 large onion, peeled and sliced. 2 shallots, finely chopped. 1 glass dry white wine. 1 egg yolk. Seasoning of salt and cayenne pepper. 4 oz. mushrooms, washed and finely sliced. Parsley stalks. ¼ pint cream. Chopped parsley. ¼ lemon.

Fillet the soles, place the bones in a saucepan, cover with water, add a few slices of onion and some parsley stalks, and bring to the boil and simmer for ½ hour, strain. Place mushrooms and shallots in a lightly-greased pan, lay in the fillet soles. Season, add white wine, fish stock, and sprinkle with chopped parsley. Cover with greaseproof paper, bring to the boil, then cook in hot oven for 8 to 10 minutes. Remove. Take out the fillets, place on a dish, keep in hot-plate. Place the stock on the fire and reduce to a glaze.

Add cream, work in the butter gradually and away from the fire, beat in the egg ; season, add a dash of lemon juice. Cover the fillets with the sauce and, before serving, brown quickly under the grill.

FILLET OF SOLE ST. GERMAIN

8 *fillets of sole. Béarnaise sauce. Fresh white bread-crumbs. 1 oz. melted butter. Seasoning of salt and pepper.*

Trim the fillets, dry well, season. Pass through the melted butter and bread-crumb. Place on a dish, season, sprinkle with melted butter and grill or cook in a hot oven until the fillets are a delicious golden-brown. Remove. Serve very hot with Béarnaise sauce piped on each fillet.

FILLET OF SOLE CUBAT

8 *fillets of sole.* $\frac{1}{8}$ *pint milk. 2 shallots. 4 oz. mushroom stalks. 1 oz. butter or margarine.* $\frac{1}{2}$ *cup grated cheese.* $\frac{1}{2}$ *oz. flour. 1 egg yolk. Seasoning of salt, pepper and cayenne pepper.*

Finely chop the shallots, wash well, and finely chop the mushroom stalks. Sweat the shallots in a little butter, add the mushrooms, season, and cook slowly until dry. Place the fillets of sole in a dish, cover with milk, season, and cook. Remove the fillets. Make a roux with $\frac{1}{2}$ oz. butter and $\frac{1}{2}$ oz. flour, add milk from the fish. Cook for 30 minutes. Strain. Add the egg yolk, mix well, stir in grated cheese, season with salt and cayenne pepper. Place the mushrooms on a serving-dish, arrange the fillets of sole along the top, pour over the sauce, sprinkle with grated cheese, and brown under the grill.

FILLET OF SOLE DUGLÈRE

*8 fillets of sole. 2 shallots, finely chopped. 6
tomatoes, skinned and chopped. ¼ pint cream.
½ bottle white wine. ½ oz. butter. Chopped parsley.
Seasoning of salt, pepper and cayenne pepper.*

Place the fillet soles in a dish, pour the wine
over them, season. Add shallots, tomatoes,
chopped parsley. Cover with greaseproof paper,
bring to the boil, then cook in the oven for 5
minutes. Remove, place the fillets on a dish,
cover, keep hot. Reduce the liquor almost to a
glaze, add cream, work in the butter, season,
pour over the fish and sprinkle with chopped
parsley.

FILLET OF SOLE ÉGYPTIENNE

*2 eggplants. 1 egg yolk. ½ oz. butter. 8 fillets of
sole. ¼ bottle dry white wine. ½ oz. flour. 2 shallots,
finely chopped. 2 tablespoons cream. 2 tomatoes,
peeled and chopped. Seasoning of salt, pepper
and cayenne pepper.*

Cut the eggplants in 2, lengthwise, mark each
slice inside with a knife (so that the flesh can
later be removed easily), fry in deep fat for 5
minutes, remove. Remove the flesh from each
slice and retain the skins. Sweat the shallots in
a little butter, add tomatoes and eggplant flesh,
season, cook until fairly dry, then replace in the
skins. Place fillets of sole in a pan, cover with
wine, season, cook on stove. Remove. Place 2
fillets on each eggplant half on a serving-dish.
Keep warm. Meanwhile, have prepared a roux
with the butter and flour, cook for 10 minutes,
add fish stock, stir well, season, and cook for 30
minutes. Remove. Add cream and egg yolk.

Pour this sauce over the fillets of sole and glaze under the grill. Serve very hot.

FILLET OF SOLE EN GOUJONS

4 *large fillets of sole. Seasoning of salt. Bread-crumbs.*

Cut the fillets of sole into thin strips, bread-crumb, fry in hot deep fat. Drain. Season to taste. Serve with Tyrolienne sauce.

SOLE OTERO

Bake 2 large potatoes. When ready, cut in two (half serves 1). Scrape out heart of potatoes ; fill with mushrooms (sliced), mussels, and shrimps mixed with shrimp sauce. Lay a poached fillet of sole on top of each. Cover with cream and cheese sauce. Sprinkle with grated Parmesan cheese and bake in the oven until browned.

SOLE SAVOYARDE

Liquor :—1 measure of red wine. 1 chopped shallot. 1 teaspoon tarragon. ½ pint fish stock.

Cover sole with the above liquor and cook in the oven for 5 or 6 minutes, according to size. Remove the sole, reduce stock till thick ; then add ¼ lb. butter in small pieces and whip ; cover sole with sliced mushrooms and peeled and chopped tomatoes. Pour sauce over the sole, glaze under the grill, then serve immediately.

SOLE MORNAY

Poach sole with dry white wine ; reduce the liquor to half and add Mornay sauce. Place sole in a baking-dish, cover with the sauce, sprinkle with grated Parmesan cheese, and brown in a very hot oven or under the grill.

SOLE FLORENTINE

Poach fillets of sole in dry white wine, then put on leaves of spinach cooked in salted water and tossed in butter or purée of spinach. Cover with Mornay sauce and sprinkle with grated Parmesan cheese and brown in a very hot oven or under the grill.

SOLE L'OSEILLE

Cooked in a similar manner as Sole Florentine, but put fillets of sole on purée of sorrel instead.

FILLET OF SOLE WALESKA

Poach fillets in dry white wine, then place on fried bread ; on each place a slice of truffle and a slice of lobster tail. Cover with Mornay sauce and glaze in the oven.

SOLE VERONIQUE

Poach fillets of sole in fish stock and 1 measure of curaçao, garnish with peeled and pipped muscat grapes, cover with reduced stock mixed with butter. Brown under the grill.

STURGEON

(Sea-water of fresh-water.) In season all the year round but rather expensive and difficult to obtain.
Long, slender, body covered with bony plates. Eggs or spawn used in preparation of caviare. Black or grey. Grey caviare favoured by gourmets. Isinglass is also obtained. Flesh may be purchased smoked and served sliced as smoked salmon.

BASIC WAYS OF COOKING

Boil (in court-bouillon or vinegar) and serve with sauce, poach. Never fry nor grill as it gets too stringy ; unless cut, flattened out like escallope of veal when it may be cooked as "Wiener Schnitzel".

POACHED STURGEON

Poach in court-bouillon and serve with hollandaise sauce.

STURGEON BORDELAISE

2 lb. fresh sturgeon (sliced). 2 oz. chopped shallots. ½ bottle red wine. 2 oz. butter. Seasoning of salt, pepper and cayenne pepper.

Grease a pan, place in the fish, sprinkle with shallots, season. Add wine. Cover with greaseproof paper and cook in the oven. When ready, remove the fish, reduce the stock by two-thirds. Take away from the fire, work in the butter, correct the seasoning, then pour the sauce over the fish.

SMOKED STURGEON

Serve sliced, with horse-radish sauce.

TROUT (truite)

(River trout and fresh-water fish.) Important game and food fish. In season all the year round. Like salmon, depends upon freshness and the shortness of time since it was caught. Has minute scales with red or dark mottlings.

BASIC WAYS OF COOKING

Bake, boil, fry, grill, steam, sauté. May be purchased smoked. (If small—serve whole; if large—may be divided through backbone and served in halves.

SMOKED TROUT

1 smoked trout (per person). 1 tomato. 1 lettuce.

Skin and remove the head of each trout, garnish with lettuce and tomato. Serve with horse-radish sauce.

*If you can obtain them alive, the best and most
delicate manner of cooking is as follows :—*

TROUT AU BLEU

1 *river trout (per person), must only be killed
at time of cooking.*

Kill, gut, roll in vinegar, pour straight away into
salted boiling water ; cook for 7 or 8 minutes.
Remove fish to a hot platter, garnish with
chopped parsley, and pass round separately
melted butter and hollandaise sauce.

TROUT MEUNIÈRE

Dip river trout in milk, then flour, sauté in butter,
season with salt. Serve on a hot platter, pour
the sauce over, sprinkle with lemon juice, and
garnish with slices of lemon and chopped parsley.

Variations :—

TROUT AMANDINE

Cooked in same way as Meunière with addition
of crushed almonds.

TROUT NIÇOISE

Cooked in same way as Meunière with addition
of chopped tomatoes, anchovies and olives.

TROUT DORIA

Cooked in same way as Meunière, garnish with
shaped cucumbers and chopped parsley.

RIVER TROUT GRENOBLOISE

4 *river trout.* 1 *oz. capers.* 2 *lemons. Butter.
Chopped parsley. Seasoning of salt and pepper.*

Flour the trouts, shallow-fry. When ready, place
on a serving-dish, sprinkle with capers, garnish

with segments of lemon free from all white pith,
chopped parsley, and season. Before serving,
pour over a little browned butter.

TUNNY

(Sea-water fish.) A giant mackerel of the Mediterranean or
Atlantic (horse-mackerel) or North Pacific (tuna).
Rich and oily. Here it is customary to purchase it tinned in oil,
but in certain areas abroad it may be purchased fresh.

BASIC WAYS OF COOKING

Fresh tunny may be braised and served with peas. Tinned
tunny fish is wonderful for hors d'œuvres, included and prepared according to one's imagination. For instance, it makes a
delightful and unusual salad :—

TUNNY FISH AND ONION

*Tunny fish, tinned in oil, sliced. Onions, peeled
and sliced finely. Vinegar.*

Mix together all ingredients in a bowl, and serve
cold.

Also, see "Vitello Tonnato", page **44**.

TURBOT

(Sea-fish.) In season all the year round.
Brown above, whitish below, and one of the best of flat-fishes.
Cut fish should be firm and close-grained and not blue. (May
be cut into steak or fillets.) If flesh is soft and bluish white, it
is not fresh.

BASIC WAYS OF COOKING

Fry, boil, braise, poach, stew, grill. Turbot *boned* may be
cooked in same manner as sole. For a party, there is not better
fish than a small turbot poached whole :—

POACHED TURBOT

Poach whole small turbot, slice and serve with
hollandaise sauce and boiled potatoes.

To carve : —Strike fish-slice along backbone, running from head to tail, and serve square slices from thick part, accompanying each slice with some gelatinous skin of fins and thin part which may be raised by laying fish-slice flat.

course ,vou mav cook the same recipe with slices of turbot!

GRILLED TURBOT

Grill the fish and serve with Tartare sauce or Maître d'Hôtel butter.

WHITEBAIT

Not fished in August and best September to March. Small fish about 2½ inches long. Delicate flavour.

BASIC WAYS OF COOKING

Shallow-fry.

WHITEBAIT DIABLÉE

1 lb. whitebait. Fried parsley. 2 lemons.

Wash well, drain, pass in a little milk, then in flour, shake off the surplus, and fry in very hot deep fat for 2 or 3 minutes. Remove. Place on a cloth, dust with salt and cayenne pepper mixed together. Serve very hot, garnish with quartered lemon and fried parsley. Accompany with brown bread and butter.

The secret of well presented whitebait is that they should be cooked and served immediately they emerge from the fat for, like the soufflé, whitebait wait for no-one!

WHITING

(Sea-water fish.) In season all the year round. Small delicately flavoured member of the cod family.

Bake, boil, fry, broil, stew. (Often fried and curled.) When served, should be cut in halves across the back and shoulder part considered the best. Cooked in the same manner as smelts.

FROGS' LEGS

There are several ways of cooking frogs' legs — Polonaise, Proven-çale, Poulette, etc. — but the most popular is the following : —

Frogs' legs are usually bought by the dozen on a stick. Prepare by trimming the ends of the legs and the ends of the backbone with sharp scissors. Remove from the stick, season with salt and pepper, dust with flour, shallow-fry in a little butter until lightly browned. Place in a dish, sprinkle with chopped parsley. Pour over the butter and serve with a quarter of lemon. If desired, a speck of garlic may be added.

Note.— The best and only way to eat and appreciate frogs' legs is to pick them up with your fingers!

SNAILS

Buy the snails already prepared or in a tin.

For service : Special plates, pincers and forks.

Butter filling : For tinned snails only. Prepared snails are ready to cook.

Crush 4 cloves of garlic, mix with 4 oz. butter, season with salt and pepper, pass through a sieve, mix with a little chopped parsley. Open the tin and drain the snails ; place one snail in each shell, fill with butter.
Prepare an old baking tray or plate with a good layer of rock salt, press in the snails and leave in a hot oven for 5 minutes. Remove. Place snails into the spaces in the plates. Serve very hot.

Note.— The tray of salt may be retained specially for this purpose indefinitely.

CAVIARE

Four kinds of sturgeon give their eggs for caviare :—Beluga (largest grains) ; Ocietrova (next sized grains) ; Sevruga (medium sized grains) ; Sterlet (smallest grains). There is black and grey caviare, and grey is the one favoured by gourmets.

There is also a "red caviare" but it has no connection with the spawn of the sturgeon for it is, in fact, salmon eggs.

The caviare which comes from Sweden, Norway and Denmark is nearly always carp eggs.

When a tin or jar of caviare is opened, it should reveal a mirror surface ; if the surface is too oily, the caviare is no good or stale.

To serve caviare :—

Serve 1 dessertspoon per person with very hot toast and half a lemon.

Americans favour caviare served with chopped onion and chopped hard-boiled egg.

Russians favour it served on blinis. Blinis is a small hot pancake with caviare spread on top and covered with sour cream.

BLINIS

2 oz. black flour. $\frac{1}{8}$ oz. yeast. 1 egg. 1 pinch of salt. Milk to mix.

Mix above ingredients into a batter and stand for 1 hour before use.

Make into pancakes roughly 4 inches across ; they should rise to $\frac{1}{2}$ inch in depth. Serve very hot.

SHELLFISH

During winter all shellfish is scarce, coarse, and not at its best; cheaper and better during spring and summer. It is customary for the fishmonger to carry out any preparations required, i.e., dressing crab, etc.

CRAB

Reddish-brown in colour. Select those which are heavy with big claws. Weight 4 to 6 lb. The shell is heavy so crab of lesser weight possesses too little meat. If possible, purchase alive.

BASIC WAYS OF COOKING

Boil (generally eaten cold).

DRESSED CRAB

1 large crab, boiled. 2 eggs, hard-boiled. 2 lettuces, quartered, shredded. Chopped parsley. Paprika. Seasoning of salt, pepper and cayenne pepper. Mayonnaise.

Remove the claws, break the shell and take off the white meat very carefully. Shred into a basin. Lift up the apron under the body with a steel and tear off. Remove the juicy substance and mix with the white meat. Season with salt, pepper, cayenne pepper and a little paprika. Mix together with a small quantity of mayonnaise. Break the shell down to the edge, wash well, dry, fill with shredded lettuce. Arrange the crab meat over the top with a flat knife. Decorate the crab and around the serving-dish to taste with egg white and yolk (pass through a fine sieve separately), chopped parsley, paprika and quartered lettuce.

Also, may be served hot; rarely cooked this way but very good :—

CRAB MORNAY

1 large crab, boiled, and flesh removed. Mornay sauce. Seasoning of salt and pepper. Grated Parmesan cheese.

At the bottom of the cleaned shell, put a little Mornay sauce ; refill with seasoned flesh ; then re-cover with Mornay sauce ; sprinkle top with grated cheese and lightly brown under a hot grill or in a hot oven.

CRAYFISH (Langouste) (Fresh-water)

Dark red when alive, bright red when boiled. Female is preferable because of roe or coral. Weight 3 to 4 lb., above this weight crayfish tends to be coarse. If possible, purchase alive.

BASIC WAYS OF COOKING

Boil, fry, sauté. (May be used in the same ways as "Lobster.")

CRAYFISH À LA RUSSE

1 large crayfish (boiled). 1 piece of stale bread, cut into a triangle—base 6 inches and height 6 inches (width of one loaf). Blanched chervil or tarragon leaves. 4 small tomatoes, skinned. 1 lettuce heart, quartered. Mayonnaise. Aspic jelly. 1 cucumber, sliced. 1 hard-boiled egg, quartered.

The shell is required for presentation so the flesh (tail only) has to be removed with care. With a sharp pair of scissors, cut away the underneath skin of the tail (both sides) and remove the flesh in one piece. Cut into ½-inch slices and place on a dish. Place the bread flat on a serving-dish to form a raised shape. Wash and dry well the shell of the crayfish, place upon the bread so that the head is well raised above the dish and the tail forms a straight slope. Mask each slice of crayfish with mayonnaise mixed with a little aspic jelly (just sufficient to set). Garnish each slice with blanched chervil or tarragon leaves ; set and coat with one layer of aspic jelly. Arrange the slices carefully, down the back of the shell and around the serving-dish. Decorate to taste with quartered lettuce heart, quartered egg, sliced cucumber, and tomatoes with the tops cut off and insides removed then filled with Russian salad. If desired, Russian salad may be served separately.

LOBSTER (Homard)

Greyish-black when alive, bright red when boiled. (If tail is straightened and springs back into place, it proves the lobster was alive when boiled.)

Female is preferable because of roe or coral. Weight 1 to 1½ lb., above this weight lobster tends to be coarse. If possible, purchase alive. Hen lobsters may be known, generally, by the spawn.

BASIC WAYS OF COOKING

Boil, fry, sauté.

DEMI HOMARD FROID

2 lobsters (½ lobster per person), boiled. 1 teaspoon capers. 1 lettuce, quartered. 2 hardboiled eggs, quartered. 2 tomatoes, peeled and quartered.

Remove claw from shell; garnish body with capers; dress on a dish with quartered lettuce, eggs and tomatoes. Serve with mayonnaise.

LOBSTER AMÉRICAINE

2 lobsters, 1 lb. each, freshly killed. ¼ pint oil. Seasoning of salt and pepper. 1 chopped shallot. 1 clove of garlic. Dab of butter. ¼ lb. butter. 1 tablespoon cream. 1 measure of brandy. ¼ pint sherry or white wine. ½ pint fish stock. 3 tomatoes, peeled and finely chopped. Tomato purée. Pinch of cayenne pepper. Chopped chervil and tarragon.

Cut off the claws and crack to ease the extraction of the flesh. Divide tail into 6 or 7 equal pieces cut up lengthwise the upper part. (Remove the greyish or dark green substance from the trunk for use in the sauce.) Heat oil in a pan until it smokes, add lobster pieces, season, and turn about until the shell reddens. Drain off oil, add shallot, garlic, brandy, sherry, fish stock, tomatoes, some tomato purée, cayenne pepper ; bring to the boil, cover and cook for $\frac{1}{4}$ hour. Remove lobster. Reduce the sauce, add greyish substance chopped with dab of butter and cook for a few seconds only. Remove from fire and finish the sauce with $\frac{1}{4}$ lb. butter, chopped chervil and tarragon, and cream ; pour sauce over lobster pieces and serve immediately.

LOBSTER CARDINALE

2 lobsters, freshly killed. 2 tablespoons oil. 2 oz. butter. 1 carrot, scraped and finely sliced. 1 onion, peeled and sliced. 3 shallots, chopped. 2 egg yolks, well beaten. 1 bay-leaf. 1 teaspoon chopped thyme and tarragon. 1 lb. tomatoes, peeled. 1 measure of brandy. 1 measure of sherry. Seasoning of salt and pepper. $\frac{1}{2}$ pint fish stock.

Split lobsters lengthwise. Put oil and butter in a sauté-pan, fry lobsters in this on both sides. When red, add vegetables, herbs, brandy, sherry, seasoning, fish stock ; cover and cook for 25 minutes. Remove lobsters. Reduce sauce, then add beaten egg yolks. Remove lobster flesh from shells and cut in slices ; replace on shells. Cover with sauce and serve immediately.

LOBSTER MORNAY

2 lobsters (cooked). Mornay sauce. Grated Gruyère cheese.

Split lobsters lengthwise ; then remove lobster flesh from shells and cut in slices. Line carcases with Mornay sauce ; replace flesh on shells. Cover with Mornay sauce, sprinkle with grated cheese, and brown under a hot grill or in a hot oven.

LOBSTER THERMIDOR

2 *lobsters, boiled and split lengthwise.* ½ *shallot.*
2 *tablespoons sherry or white wine.* ¼ *teaspoon*
English mustard. Chopped parsley. ¼ *pint thick*
cream. Grated Gruyère cheese.

Remove lobster flesh from shells and cut in slices.
Then fry in a small sauté-pan the shallot with
the sherry, mustard and parsley. Cook for 5 or
6 minutes or until sherry is reduced to half. Add
cream. Stir in lobster pieces. Then refill shells
with this mixture, sprinkle with grated cheese
and lightly brown under a hot grill.

LOBSTER NEWBURG

2 *lobsters (female),* 1 *lb. each (live).* 1 *measure*
of sherry. 1 *cup water.* 1 *oz. butter.* ¼ *pint cream.*
Seasoning of salt, pepper and cayenne pepper.

Remove claws and tail ; slice the body down the
centre and remove the coral.
Place butter in a pan and melt until a light brown.
Put in the pieces of lobster, and fry until both
sides of them are red ; add sherry, water, season,
cover and cook for 10 minutes. Remove lobsters,
strain, reduce until only a little stock remains ;
add cream and re-boil. Pound the coral until a
smooth paste is obtained ; add coral to the sauce.
Do not re-boil. Correct seasoning. Take lobsters
from the shell, place in a dish, strain the sauce
on top. Serve with a Rice Pilaff.

LOBSTER XAVIER

2 *lobsters, boiled.* 2 *oz. mushrooms, finely sliced.*
Butter. ¼ *pint cream.* 1 *egg yolk. Pinch of mustard,*
diluted. Seasoning of salt and pepper.

Remove the lobster claws and cut in 2, lengthwise. Remove the flesh from the claws and body,

cut into ½-inch dice. Heat a piece of butter in a pan, add mushrooms and cook for 1 minute, add diced lobsters, lightly toss, season. Add cream and diluted mustard, season, simmer for 5 minutes. Remove. Place the lobster meat in the shells. To the sauce add egg yolk, then pour sauce over the lobster. Glaze under the grill. Serve very hot.

BISQUE DE HOMARD

2 lobsters (live), split lengthwise. 3 oz. butter. 2 tablespoons oil. 1 onion, peeled and chopped. 1 carrot, scraped and sliced. 1 stick of celery, chopped. Pinch of thyme. Parsley stalks. 2 bay-leaves. 1 measure of brandy. 1 measure of sherry or white wine. 1½ lb. tomatoes, peeled and chopped. 3 oz. tomato purée. ¼ teaspoon chopped tarragon. 1 quart fish stock. Seasoning of salt and pepper. 2 oz. butter ; 1 measure sherry ; 1 cup cream (thick).

Put in a pan—3 oz. butter and oil, add onion, carrot, celery, bay-leaves, thyme and a few parsley stalks. Add lobsters and fry. When lobsters redden, flambé with the brandy, then add sherry. Add tomatoes, tomato purée, tarragon, fish stock. Cook slowly. Season. After boiling for 20 minutes, remove lobsters and let remainder cook until soft. Pass sauce through a sieve and tammy cloth and reduce to the right thickness. Remove from fire, add 2 oz. butter, sherry, cream, and flesh from the lobsters cut into small dice. Serve very hot.

SHRIMPS AND PRAWNS

In season all the year round, but cannot be fished during excessively bad weather, and a bad traveller in excessively hot weather. Pale greyish transparent colour with brown spots and pinkish-brown when boiled. Customarily purchased boiled. Fresh shrimps and prawns should be firm and crisp. Shrimps are small and long-tailed. Prawns are similar but larger. Scampi is really a large prawn found mostly in the Adriatic Sea, so here Dublin Bay prawns are used as a substitute for scampi.

BASIC WAYS OF COOKING

Fry, sauté, grill.

Note.—Very popular served shelled with fine slices of brown bread and butter. Potted shrimps delicious with buttered toast.

PRAWN COCKTAIL

1 *pint large prawns, shelled.* 1 *lettuce.*

Place in bottom of each person's bowl a little finely-shredded lettuce with a few prawns on top. Serve separately a sauce composed of half mayonnaise and half tomato ketchup, mixed well together and seasoned with cayenne pepper.

SHRIMP COCKTAIL

1 *pint shelled shrimps.* 1 *lettuce, shredded.*

Place in bottom of each person's bowl a little finely-shredded lettuce with a few shrimps on top. Serve separately a sauce composed of half mayonnaise, half tomato ketchup, dash of Worcester sauce mixed well together and seasoned with cayenne pepper.

PILAFF DE LANGOUSTINE

6 *large Dublin Bay prawns per person (shell raw), or crayfish with flesh removed and cut into large dice. Butter.* 1 *measure of brandy.* 1 *measure of sherry.* ¼ *pint cream. Stewed rice.*

Fry prawns in butter in a small saucepan, add brandy and sherry, cover with cream. Boil slowly for about 10 minutes until it thickens and serve with stewed rice.

FRIED SCAMPI

6 *large Dublin Bay prawns per person (shell raw). Sprig of parsley, fried. Seasoning of salt and pepper. ¼ lemon per person. Sprinkling of milk and flour.*

Pass prawns in a little milk, roll in flour and fry in deep fat. Drain, season. Garnish with fired parsley and quartered lemon. Serve very hot with Tartare sauce.

GRILLED SCAMPI

6 *Dublin Bay prawns per person (shell raw). Maître d'Hôtel butter. Seasoning of salt and pepper.*

Stuff prawns with Maître d'Hôtel butter, skewer, season, then grill. Serve immediately they are ready.

SCAMPI NAPOLITAINE

24 *large Dublin Bay prawns (shell raw). ⅛ pint oil. 2 sections garlic. 1 dessertspoon tomato purée. Seasoning of salt, pepper and cayenne pepper. 1 measure white wine. 6 tomatoes, peeled and chopped. 2 shallots, finely chopped.*

Heat oil in a pan, add scampi and fry quickly, turning over and over for 5 minutes. Add shallots and garlic, cook for 1 minute. Add white wine, tomatoes and tomato purée, season, and cook for 10 minutes slowly. Remove the garlic, correct the seasoning, and serve with risotto.

MOLLUSCS

In season when there is an "R" in the month.

MUSSELS (Moules)

(Fresh-water or sea-water.) Should be well closed until cooked, then shells open automatically.

BASIC WAYS OF COOKING

Fry, stew.

MUSSELS MARINIÈRE

3 *pints mussels.* ½ *bottle dry white wine.* 1 *oz. butter.* 4 *shallots, finely chopped.* *Chopped parsley.* *Seasoning of salt and pepper.*

Scrub and wash mussels in several changes of cold water, drain, place in saucepan with the shallots, wine, some parsley, butter, seasoning. Cover tightly and boil for 10 minutes (shaking the saucepan occasionally) until the mussels open. Drain stock gently into another pan, meanwhile taste for seasoning and reduce. Dress the mussels in the half shells and place in a dish. Pour the sauce over the mussels. Sprinkle with chopped parsley. If desired, a little cream may be added to the sauce ; or roux to the boiling stock.
The mussel shells act as "spoons", so each person should have an extra plate for the empty shells.

MOULEVALENCIA (The Spanish Dish)

2 *pints mussels, scrubbed and washed.* ⅛ *pint olive oil.* *Clove of garlic.* *Water.* *Bouquet garni.* *Boiled rice.*

Gently fry mussels in olive oil with garlic ; do not allow to cook completely, only until *just* opening. Then bring to the boil in water to which is added liquid from frying-pan, with bouquet garni. (Shredded lobsters, shrimps, prawns, may be added.) Reduce liquid by a third, then pour all over boiled rice. Serve at once.

OYSTERS

(Sea-water.) English oysters are famous for their good qualities; those from Whitstable, Brightlingsea and Colchester being well-known varieties. Oyster-beds at Inveraray and Ballantrae in Scotland, and at Wicklow and Queenstown in Ireland produce oysters of excellent quality too. A fresh oyster has a firmly closed shell; when shell is open, the oyster is dead and unfit to eat. Flesh should be firm and white or cream colour. Best size is $3\frac{1}{2}$ to $3\frac{3}{4}$ inches in diameter. Beard should be of light brown or sandy colour, although in some areas it is green. (Fishmonger will open them for you or show you how to open them.)

BASIC WAYS OF COOKING

Fry, stew. Also used for soup (oyster soup).

Raw oysters (carefully open to retain juice, remove upper shell and leave in deeper half) are served with accompaniments of lemon, vinegar, red pepper and other relishes, and finely sliced brown bread and butter.

Following recipe mainly used as garnish for fish or rump steak:—

FRIED OYSTERS

(Large oysters are best for this recipe). Simmer for 2 minutes in own liquor; drain very well; dip in egg yolk and then bread-crumb; season with salt, cayenne pepper and nutmeg, and fry until lightly browned.
If you desire to make this recipe a main dish— moisten melted butter with oyster liquor and serve as sauce.

OYSTER STEW

Melt a knob of butter and gently cook with 1 dessertspoon flour; do not colour. Add 1 pint milk and cook, stirring continually. Add oysters, $\frac{1}{2}$ pint cream and seasoning of salt and cayenne pepper.

OYSTER SOUP

Drain liquor from 1½ dozen oysters, strain through muslin cloth and retain. Meanwhile, bring 1 pint milk to the boil. Heat oysters in their liquor until edges begin to ruffle, then pour milk over them. Add ½ pint cream. Keep hot but do not boil. Season with salt and cayenne pepper. Just before serving, stir in knob of butter. Serve with small oyster crackers.

CLAMS

Raw clams may be served in their shells with accompaniments of lemon, vinegar, red pepper and other relishes.

SCALLOPS

(Sea-fish.) Fan-shaped shells, orangy red and with albumen-like whites.

BASIC WAYS OF COOKING

Fry, stew. (Shallow-fry and serve with bacon.)

ST. JACQUES BONNE-FEMME

(Serves 4 people.)

12 scallops, cut in 2. 4 oz. button mushrooms, well washed and sliced. 2 chopped shallots. ¼ bottle dry white wine. Seasoning of salt, pepper and cayenne pepper. ½ teaspoon lemon juice. Chopped parsley. 2 egg yolks. ¼ pint cream.

Place scallops, sliced mushrooms, shallots in a saucepan ; add white wine, seasoning ; bring to the boil, cover and simmer slowly for 15 minutes. Remove the scallops. Reduce the remainder of the stock to nearly a glacé, add cream, re-heat, add egg yolks. DO NOT RE-BOIL. Work in 1 oz. butter. Correct seasoning. Add lemon juice and chopped parsley.

Arrange scallops in 4 shells, pour over the sauce, and brown quickly under the grill. Serve very hot.

SCALLOPS MEUNIÈRE

Allow 3 scallops per person. 1 oz. butter. Seasoning of salt and pepper. 1 lemon. Chopped parsley.

Clean scallops, cut in 2 lengthwise, scour. Roll in flour and shallow-fry until brown. Place on a serving-dish, garnish with chopped parsley and slices of lemon. Brown butter in a pan and pour over the scallops. Serve very hot.

REMNANTS

COQUILLE OF FISH

Obtain a few large scallop shells from your fishmonger. Mashed potatoes. Mornay or Béchamel sauce. Any left-over cooked mixed fish. Grated Parmesan cheese.

Surround the shells with the mashed potatoes, fill the centres with the mixed fish at your disposal, cover with chosen sauce; bake in the oven for 8 to 10 minutes, remove, sprinkle with grated cheese, and glaze under a hot grill before serving.

FISH CAKES

½ lb. cooked fish, flaked or minced. 1 teaspoon anchovy essence. Seasoning of salt and pepper. ¼ lb. mashed potatoes. 1 tablespoon melted butter. Milk. 2 cups bread-crumbs.

Mix fish with potatoes, anchovy essence and butter, season; shape into flat cakes, dip in milk and bread-crumbs and fry in hot fat.

If preferred, cakes may be dusted with flour and placed on a baking sheet in a hot oven to brown instead of fry.

Drain cakes on draining-tray and serve on a hot platter garnished with fried parsley.

FISH CROQUETTES

½ lb. cooked fish, flaked or minced. ½ lb. hot mashed potatoes. Seasoning of salt and pepper, 1 egg, well beaten. 2 cups bread-crumbs. Fried parsley.

Mix fish and potatoes, season, then shape into rounds, and coat with egg and bread-crumbs, and fry in hot fat. Garnish with fried parsley before serving.

FISH TURBAN

1 *lb. cooked fish, flaked.* 1½ *cups milk.* 1 *onion, peeled and sliced. Blade of mace. Sprig of parsley.* ¼ *cup butter.* ¼ *cup flour. Seasoning of salt and pepper. Dash of lemon juice.* 2 *egg yolks, beaten.* ½ *cup bread-crumbs.*

Scald milk with onion, parsley and mace ; remove onion and herbs. Melt butter, add flour, season, and slowly stir in milk. Bring to boiling point and add egg yolks. Layer a buttered dish with the fish, season, add lemon juice ; cover with sauce. Repeat this procedure, shaping gradually into pyramid form. Sprinkle with bread-crumbs and bake in hot oven until browned.

FISH AU GRATIN

1 *cup cooked fish, flaked.* 1 *cup bread-crumbs. Seasoning of salt and pepper.* 1 *cup white sauce. Grated Parmesan cheese.*

Heat the fish in white sauce, season, then pour into buttered baking dish ; cover with bread-crumbs and grated cheese. Bake in a hot oven until golden brown.

FISH À LA PROVENÇALE

¼ *cup butter.* 2 *tablespoons flour.* 2 *cups milk.* 4 *yolks of hard-boiled eggs, mashed.* 1 *teaspoon anchovy sauce.* 2 *cups cooked fish, flaked. Toast.*

Stir butter, flour and milk together ; mix anchovy sauce with mashed egg yolks, then add to butter, flour, milk. Add fish, and bring to boiling point. Serve immediately on hot toast.

FISH CURRY

½ *lb. cooked white fish, flaked.* 1 *dessertspoon curry powder.* 1 *onion, finely chopped. A little*

147

chopped chutney. 1 oz. sultanas. 1 oz. margarine or butter. 1 dessertspoon flour. ½ pint stock. Seasoning of salt and pepper. Boiled rice or mashed potato.

Heat butter and fry onion lightly in it without colouring; stir in flour and curry powder, cook slowly for 5 minutes, then stir in stock slowly; bring to the boil, season, stirring continually; add sultanas, and simmer for 15 minutes. Then add fish and chutney and heat together. Serve in centre of a hot platter and surround with boiled rice or mashed potato.

A variety of accompaniments may be served with curry, such as sliced banana, grated coconut, chopped almonds. Pass round separately Bombay ducks and puppodums and chutney, or other relishes.

FISH CUSTARD

Cooked fish (skin and bones removed), or tinned salmon may be used. 2 eggs, well beaten. ½ pint warm milk. Seasoning of salt and pepper.

Layer a buttered or greased baking-dish with the fish, season. Meanwhile, add warm milk to beaten eggs, then pour this over the fish. Cook in a moderate oven for approximately 35 minutes or until set. Serve immediately.

FISH SOUFFLÉ

2 cups cooked fish, rinsed and flaked. Seasoning of salt and paprika. 2 teaspoons lemon juice. ½ cup bread-crumbs. ½ cup milk. 3 egg yolks, beaten until thick. 3 egg whites.

Season the fish. Cook bread-crumbs in milk for 5 minutes, remove, add fish and egg yolks beaten well; then fold in egg whites; beat until stiff. Turn into buttered dish, set in pan of hot water

and bake bain-marie until firm. (Moderate oven.)
If desired, serve with Spanish sauce.

FISH HASH

½ *lb. cooked fish, flaked.* ½ *lb. boiled potatoes,
finely chopped. Seasoning of salt and pepper.
Fat.*

Heat fat in a frying-pan, put in the fish and
potatoes, stir until heated then cook until lightly
browned underneath ; fold, and turn like an
omelet.

FISH GALANTINE

1 *lb. cooked fish, flaked. Egg or anchovy sauce.
1 egg yolk, beaten. 1 egg white. 1 lb. cooked sieved
potatoes. 1 dessertspoon chopped parsley. Seasoning of salt and pepper. Bread-crumbs.*

Bind fish with sauce, parsley, potatoes, seasoning, and egg yolk. Shape into a large sausage.
Place on a greased baking sheet, brush with egg
white, sprinkle with bread-crumbs and bake in
a moderate oven until browned.
May be eaten hot or cold. If cold, serve with a
seasonal green salad.

With fried fish left-overs :—

FISH MOLEY (An Indian breakfast dish)

1 *lb. fried fish. 1 small onion, peeled and sliced.
2 oz. sliced green ginger. 3 or 4 sliced green chillies
or capsicums.* ½ *teaspoon saffron. Juice of 1 lemon.*
¼ *lb. desiccated coconut, covered with boiling
water and left until required. (If possible, use
instead milk of* ½ *coconut.) Boiled rice. 2 oz.
fat or dripping.*

Fry onion in fat (in a saucepan), add green ginger,
fish, chillies and saffron. Stir in strained coconut

water and lemon juice. Cook on a slow fire for 10 minutes, or until it thickens a little. Serve with boiled rice.

FISH PUDDING

$\frac{1}{2}$ *lb. cooked fish, flaked. 1 oz. melted butter.* $\frac{1}{4}$ *pint milk. 1 teaspoon chopped parsley. 2 tablespoons bread-crumbs. 1 oz. flour. 1 egg, well beaten. Seasoning of salt and pepper.*

Grease a basin and sprinkle with bread-crumbs ; add fish with flour, parsley, seasoning ; then mix with egg, melted butter and milk. Pour into prepared mould, cover with greaseproof paper and steam for 30 to 40 minutes. Serve immediately with any fish sauce desired.

FISH TIMBALES

2 cups cooked fish chopped finely. $\frac{1}{4}$ *cup thick cream, beaten stiff. Seasoning of salt and cayenne pepper.* $1\frac{1}{2}$ *teaspoons lemon juice. 3 egg whites. Béchamel sauce. Chopped parsley.*

Season fish, add lemon juice ; then add cream and egg whites. Stir well, and turn into small buttered moulds. Cover moulds with greaseproof paper and bake them bain-marie in a moderate oven for 20 minutes. When ready, remove from moulds, cover with Béchamel sauce and garnish with chopped parsley before serving.

GEFILLTE FISH (FISH BALLS) (An Israeli dish)

1 lb. mixed cooked fish (herring, cod, haddock, etc.), boned and skinned. 2 onions, peeled. 1 large carrot, scraped. 1 pint water. Seasoning of salt and pepper. 1 slice of stale bread, soaked in water and drained. 1 egg, beaten well.

Put fish in saucepan with 1 onion and the carrot ;
pour in the water, season, and let simmer for 20
minutes ; strain, and reserve the stock and carrot.
Put fish, remaining onion and soaked bread
through mincing machine. Correct seasoning.
Bind with beaten egg, and shape the mixture
into balls. Bring fish stock to the boil, drop in
the fish balls, and let simmer gently for 1 hour.
When ready, remove the balls carefully, serve on
a hot platter and garnish each with a slice of
cooked carrot.

HADDOCK PATTIES

*¼ lb. cooked smoked haddock, flaked. 1 oz. grated
cheese. ¼ oz. butter or margarine. ¼ oz. flour.
¼ pint milk. Short or flaky pastry. Seasoning of
salt and pepper. Chopped parsley.*

Melt butter, stir in flour, add milk and bring to
the boil whilst stirring. Add fish with grated
cheese and parsley. Cook for a minute and allow
to cool. Roll pastry into rounds and place some
of the mixture on to each round. Dampen edges,
fold over the pastry, seal the edges. Brush with
eggwash. Bake for approximately ½ hour.

HADDOCK AND MACARONI PIE

*½ lb. cooked smoked haddock. 2 oz. cooked macaroni.
½ pint white sauce. Grated rind of 1 lemon. ¼
oz. dripping. Bread-crumbs. Seasoning of salt
and pepper.*

Layer alternately fish and macaroni in buttered
pie-dish. Add lemon rind and seasoning to white
sauce and pour over fish. Sprinkle with bread-
crumbs, top with dripping and bake until
browned.

KEDGEREE

1 *lb. cooked fish (boned and skinned), flaked.*
½ *lb. boiled rice.* 1 *hard-boiled egg, chopped.* 1 *oz.*
butter or margarine. Seasoning of salt and pepper.
Chopped parsley.

Melt butter in pan, add all ingredients, and heat.
Serve on a hot platter and garnish with chopped
egg and chopped parsley.

Lobster remnants turn into excellent dishes:—

LOBSTER FARCI

1 *cup chopped cooked lobster meat.* 2 *hard-*
boiled egg yolks. ½ *tablespoon chopped parsley.*
1 *cup white sauce. Pinch of grated nutmeg.* ¼
cup bread-crumbs. Seasoning of salt and pepper.
Lobster shells.

Add egg yolks to lobster meat rubbed to paste,
parsley, sauce, and seasoning to taste. Fill the
lobster shells, cover with buttered bread-crumbs,
and bake until browned.

LOBSTER AND OYSTER RAGOÛT

¼ *cup butter*; ¼ *cup flour*; ¾ *cup oyster liquor*;
¾ *cup cream*; ½ *teaspoon salt*; *few grains cayenne*;
few drops onion juice; ¼ *teaspoon pepper.*
1 *pint oysters.* 1 *cup cooked lobster dice.* ½ *measure*
of dry white wine. 1 *tablespoon parsley, finely*
chopped.

Parboil oysters (put clean oysters in saucepan
with water and liquor drained from them, heat
and cook until oysters are plumb and edges begin
to curl, drain, add water to make oyster liquor;
strain). Make sauce of first 8 ingredients; then
add oysters, lobster dice, wine and chopped
parsley. Serve immediately.

LOBSTER FRICASSÉE

2 *lb. cooked lobster, cut into strips.* ¼ *cup butter.*
¾ *lb. mushrooms, peeled and diced.* ½ *teaspoon
onion juice.* 1 *measure of sherry.* ¼ *cup flour.* 1½
cups milk. Seasoning of salt and paprika.

Cook butter with mushrooms and onion juice
for 4 minutes; add flour and stir in milk slowly.
Add lobster meat, season, and add sherry just
before serving.

LOBSTER NEWBURG

2 *lb. cooked lobsters.* 1 *measure of sherry.* 1
cup water. 1 *oz. butter.* ¼ *pint cream. Seasoning
of salt, pepper and cayenne pepper.*

Cut lobsters into suitable pieces, lightly fry in
butter, add sherry and cream. Cover, simmer
slowly, colour a light pink with vegetable colouring. Serve with a rice pilaff.

*Newburg sauce may be used for practically any re-heated food besides lobster — all
kinds of fish, meat, game, eggs, vegetables.*

SALMON OR TUNNYFISH LOAF

2 *cups cooked salmon, flaked, or tunnyfish.*
½ *cup bread-crumbs.* 4 *tablespoons butter.* 2 *eggs,
beaten.* 1 *tablespoon chopped parsley. Seasoning
of salt and pepper.*

Mix ingredients together well and steam for 1
hour in a buttered mould, or bake bain-marie in
a moderate oven. Serve hot or cold. If cold,
serve with a seasonal salad.

SALMON MAYONNAISE

*Slices of cooked salmon. Lettuce, finely shred-
ded (or one of the winter salads, i.e., curly endive,*

*batavia, etc.). 2 tomatoes, peeled and quartered.
Mayonnaise sauce. Capers. 2 hardboiled eggs,
sliced.*

Place salmon on a bed of finely shredded lettuce ;
cover with mayonnaise sauce ; decorate edges of
bowl with tomatoes and eggs ; sprinkle with a
few capers.

SCALLOPED COD WITH OYSTERS

*½ lb. cooked cod, flaked. Seasoning of salt and
pepper. Oysters. Melted butter. Seasoning of
lemon juice and cayenne pepper. Bread-crumbs.
½ cup oyster liquor or water. Hollandaise sauce.*

Layer buttered baking-dish with fish, season.
cover with oysters dipped in melted butter,
season with lemon juice and cayenne, sprinkle
with bread-crumbs ; moisten with oyster liquor.
Repeat this procedure and finally cover with
bread-crumbs. Bake for 20 minutes in a hot
oven and serve with Hollandaise sauce.

BASIC METHODS OF COOKING FISH

AU GRATIN

Covered with sauce, topped with bread-crumbs and grated
cheese, browned under the grill or in a hot oven.

BAKE

(If **whole fish** to be cooked, wash and wipe with a clean cloth,
cut off head and fins and truss—
If **fish steaks or fillets** to be cooked, wash and wipe dry, season,
dust with flour and sprinkle with lemon juice, or coat with egg
and bread-crumbs.)
May be baked in a tin with spices and butter or in milk. Cover
with greased paper and bake in moderate oven for 10—30
minutes, according to size. (Fillets 10—15 minutes.) Drain

before **serving**. Serve with cut lemon, parsley, anchovy or parsley sauce.

BOIL

(Suitable for large, round fish or thick pieces and is best way to cook salt fish.)

Wash and wipe fish and place in saucepan; water should simmer, NOT BOIL, and only enough used to cover fish. Add dessertspoon lemon juice or vinegar to water to keep fish white and firm and add salt unless it is salt fish. (Believe it or not, sea-water is excellent for boiling sweet fish!) Allow 5 minutes to the lb. for thin fish, 10 minutes or more for larger fish. Serve with cut lemon, parsley, melted butter or egg, anchovy or parsley sauce.

FRY

(Suitable for lean fish.) Trim, wash, wipe **dry**, and **dust fish** with flour; fry in a bath of boiling fat, dripping, lard or oil, or shallowfry in a little hot fat or butter in a frying-pan. Melt fat slowly in pan until it becomes *smoking hot* before placing in fish. Turn food with a knife and never pierce with a fork; drain for fried fish must be perfectly dry, and serve with a sauce or else with lemon or vinegar.

GRILL or BROIL

(Suitable for oily fish.) Trim, wash, wipe dry, and dust fish with flour, or brush with melted butter or olive oil. Put on a greased gridiron. If thick (like mackerel), split fish down the centre and grill the flesh side first. (Remove head and tail for grilling.) Place under grill for 2 or 3 minutes until golden, then cook other side in same way. Serve with a dab of parsley butter.
Parsley butter—chopped parsley, lemon juice, seasoning, with butter.

PLANKED

Planked fish is grilled and served on a board made for this purpose.

POACH

Prepare and heat fish stock (with left-over fish bones) in a pan and lower fish into it. Cook gently for approximately 20 minutes. Drain, keep hot; meanwhile, make a sauce from liquor, a little milk and flour to thicken.

SAUTÉ

Cook in small quantity of fat or butter in saucepan, then turn over and cook other side; lower heat and cook slowly until done, shaking pan constantly.

SOUSE

(Suitable for mackerel, herring.) Put slice of onion on each fillet, roll up, put into a casserole, add sprinkling of sugar, good sprinkling of pepper and a pinch of mixed spice, 1 teaspoon peppercorns and cloves, couple of bay-leaves and good pinch of mustard, then cover fish with vinegar. Cover, and cook very slowly in the oven until tender.

STEAM

(Better than boiling because less juice is extracted, but takes a little longer.) Wash and wipe fish and place in steamer. (Allow 15 minutes to lb. and 15 minutes over.) Small fillets of fish may be steamed on greased plate covered with another plate over a pan of boiling water. (Allow 20 to 30 minutes.) Squeeze lemon juice over to keep flesh white. Serve with cut lemon, parsley, melted butter or egg, anchovy or parsley sauce.

Drain away all water or grease before serving.
If fish leaves the bone easily or skin starts cracking, it is cooked!
And if your hands smell "fishy" after handling fish, try rubbing a spoonful of mustard into your hands then giving them a good wash!

SAUCES

"Tell me how you eat
And I will tell you
Who you are."

BRILLAT-SAVARIN

Just as a plain dress is
transformed into a chic model
by accessories of good taste, so
the plainest food is transformed
into a gourmet's dish by a
well made sauce.

But, truly to appreciate the
magic of a sauce—whether
savoury or sweet—it is essential
to make it yourself. Only by
your own effort, skill and
patience (the preparation of a
sauce requires more care and
attention than is generally
realized), can you discover how
wonderful and exciting is
its creation.

The result turns an ordinary
recipe into a refined art—adds
zest to the appetite—and is the
finishing touch of the
master in the culinary world!

1. WHITE SAUCE

2. BROWN SAUCE

3. SAUCE WITH AN OIL BASIS

There are three sauce classifications. ("Unclassified" sauces, such as apple sauce, bread sauce, etc., are really accompaniments.)

The following are the white and brown sauce foundations :—

ROUX. A thickening agent which combines equal parts of flour and butter or fat cooked together.

WHITE ROUX (for white sauces, soups, etc.) Cook slowly and do not allow to colour.

BROWN ROUX (for brown sauces, also stews, soups, etc.)

Cook until a natural rich brown colour is obtained.

WHITE STOCK OR FOND BLANC (for white sauces and soups) Place bones available (beef, lamb or veal) into a saucepan. Boil. Skim well, add sliced carrots and onions, celery, leeks, herbs, peppercorns. Cook for 2 to 3 hours. Strain.

BROWN STOCK (for brown sauces, also stews, soups, roast gravy, etc.)

Place bones available (beef, lamb or veal) into a roasting tray. Add sliced onion and carrot and a bouquet garni. Brown in the oven. Remove. Drain off the fat. Place the bones and the vegetables into a saucepan. Cover with water, boil, skim, add a little salt and a few peppercorns. Cook slowly for 2 to 3 hours. Strain.

COURT BOUILLON (short broth, mainly used for fish and excellent for trout, eel)

2 quarts cold water. ¾ cup red wine or vinegar or dry white wine. Salt to taste. 2 small carrots, scraped and sliced. 2 small onions, peeled and thinly sliced. 1 bouquet garni. ½ teaspoon peppercorns, slightly bruised.

Place all the above ingredients in a pan, bring to a boil, let simmer gently for a few minutes ; bring to a boil again ; add fish or meat ; lower heat and simmer gently until fish or meat is tender.

FISH STOCK (for fish sauces)

Use fish bones. Cover with cold water. Boil, skim, add sliced onions, leeks, celery, thyme and bay - leaf, peppercorns. Cook for 45 minutes. Strain.

WHITE SAUCE (for boiled or steamed vegetables, fish, white meat, poultry, etc., and white sauces generally)

1½ oz. butter or margarine. 1½ oz. flour. ½ pint milk, or milk and water, or milk and stock/vegetable water. Seasoning of salt and pepper.

Melt butter in saucepan over low heat, add flour, stir for 5 minutes but do not brown. Add one-third of the liquid, stirring continually until boiling ; gradually add remainder of liquid and continue boiling slowly for 30 to 35 minutes. Season.

WHITE SAUCE (without fat)

1 oz. flour. ½ peeled onion. 2 cloves. 1 gill milk. 3 gills water. Seasoning of salt and pepper.

Put flour into a basin and work till smooth with wooden spoon, with 2 tablespoons water ; put remainder of water, milk and onion with cloves stuck in it, into a pan ; bring to the boil and strain on to blended flour, stirring well. Return to pan and re-heat, stirring continually. Season and let simmer for 5 minutes.

White sauce variations :—

ANCHOVY SAUCE (serve with fish, eggs)

As white sauce (without fat) but add anchovy essence to taste.

CAPER SAUCE (serve with boiled mutton, fish)

As white sauce (without fat) but add 2 teaspoons caper vinegar and 3 dessertspoons capers ; simmer for 3 minutes.

CHEESE SAUCE

As white sauce but, when ready, add 1 cup grated cheese and stir over stove till melted.

EGG SAUCE

As white sauce (without fat) but add chopped hard-boiled egg.

ONION SAUCE (serve with roast or boiled shoulder of lamb, mutton, fish)

As white sauce (without fat) but, when ready, stir into it 4 onions boiled till soft, strained and chopped finely ; simmer for 5 minutes.

PARSLEY SAUCE

As white sauce (without fat) but add 1 tablespoon chopped parsley.

BROWN SAUCE

To make 1 pint brown sauce :—

2 oz. fat. 1 onion. Bouquet garni. Dash of salt and pepper. 2 oz. flour. 1 carrot. 1 dessertspoon of tomato purée. 1½ pints brown stock.

Heat the fat and add diced vegetables. Cook for 5 minutes. Stir in the flour. Cook for 5 minutes or until brown. Stir in brown stock. Add seasoning, tomato purée and bouquet garni. Simmer 1½ to 2 hours. Strain. (Cook this sauce well, long, slow, and skimming is very important while simmering as all traces of fat should be removed.)

For light-brown sauce :—

Add 2 tablespoons cream before straining.

Note. —This is a most interesting sauce for it is not only a foundation brown sauce and used for stews, minces, sautés, but, with the addition of 1 glass of sherry or Madeira, may be served with steak, tongue, hamburger, sausage, ham ; or, with the addition of 1 glass of port, may be served with duck, wild duck, teal, etc. Alternatively, with the addition of finely shredded orange or tangerine rind and orange juice plus 1 glass of sherry, may be served with duck and the duck decorated with the segments of orange.

Example recipe using brown sauce :—

DUCK AUX CERISES

1 young duck. 2 tablespoons sugar. 1 dessertspoon redcurrant jelly. 1 lb. stoned cherries. Brown sauce. 1 measure or glass of marsala. Seasoning of salt and pepper.

Roast the duck ; allow 1 to 1½ hours. Cut into portions and place on heated dish. Place cherries and sugar in a saucepan and cook until a brown colour. Decorate the duck with cherries along the centre and around the serving dish, and keep hot in the oven. Add crushed nuts (removed from the cherry-stones), redcurrant jelly and marsala to the brown sauce, let simmer slowly for 10 minutes. Strain. Correct seasoning and pour sauce over the duck before serving.

And here are the special foundation sauces :—

BÉCHAMEL SAUCE (A white sauce—unwise to prepare this in advance as it is a rich white sauce)

$\frac{1}{2}$ *pint stock.* $\frac{1}{2}$ *pint milk. Carrot, onion, celery* 1 *bay-leaf.* 2 *oz. butter.* 2 *oz. flour.* 10 *pepper-corns.*

Simmer vegetables, stock and seasoning for 10 minutes ; melt butter, add flour, cook for 5 minutes ; add milk and stock (strained). Cook for 30 minutes. Strain.

Béchamel sauce variation :—

AURORE SAUCE (serve with eggs, poultry, etc.) Béchamel sauce blended with tomato sauce to colour it orange-pink.

VELOUTÉ SAUCE (a white sauce—may be prepared in advance and stored until required in refrigerator)

3 *tablespoons flour.* 2 *tablespoons butter.* 1 *pint white stock.* $\frac{1}{2}$ *teaspoon lemon juice.* $\frac{1}{2}$ *cup cream. Seasoning of salt and pepper.*

Melt the butter, stir in the flour and cook for 5 minutes ; stir in stock and simmer for 30 minutes. Whisk until a stiff consistency is obtained ; season and add cream.

Note.—For Chicken Velouté use chicken stock, for Veal Velouté use veal stock, for Fish Velouté use fish stock.

Velouté sauce variations :—

SUPRÊME SAUCE

Prepare Velouté sauce but stock used must be chicken broth. Just before serving, stir in 2 egg yolks.

ALLEMANDE SAUCE

Add 1 cup grated Parmesan cheese to Suprême sauce.

MUSHROOM SAUCE

Prepare Velouté sauce and add 4 sliced mushrooms ; cook for 5 minutes, season. If desired, 1 chopped truffle may be added.

ESPAGNOLE SAUCE (Spanish sauce) (a brown sauce—for fish, eggs, poultry, game, meats or vegetables)

2 tablespoons finely chopped lean raw ham or bacon. 2 tablespoons chopped carrot. 4 tablespoons butter. 1½ cups brown stock. 2 tablespoons chopped celery. 1 tablespoon chopped onion. 4 tablespoons flour. ⅔ cup stewed tomatoes.

Cook ham or bacon and vegetables with butter until butter is browned ; add flour and stir ; cook for 5 minutes ; add stock and tomatoes ; cook for 35 minutes and strain.

Another foundation sauce worth knowing is :—

PANADA (for croquettes, also soufflés, etc.)

This is a thick binding sauce made in the proportion of 1 oz. fat to 1 oz. flour to ¼ pint liquid.

APPLE SAUCE (serve with roast pork, roast duck, roast goose)

¼ lb. of apples. ½ oz. margarine or butter. 1 teaspoon sugar.

Peel and core the apples ; cut in quarters. Place in saucepan with sugar, cover with water and cook slowly until soft. Add margarine. Beat well. Pour into sauceboat.

BACON ROLLS (serve with roast game, roast poultry)

Cut some finely sliced bacon into lengths of about 2 to 3 inches. Stretch lengthwise with a knife. Roll up and thread on a skewer. Bake for 5 to 10 minutes. Use for a garnish or as an accompaniment to roast game and roast poultry.

BÉARNAISE SAUCE (excellent with all grills, even fried fish, but customarily served with beef)

2 egg yolks. ¼ lb. melted butter or margarine. 2 dessertspoons vinegar (tarragon vinegar may be used). 1 oz. tarragon leaves, chopped. 1 shallot, chopped. 12 grains of crushed peppercorns. Seasoning of cayenne pepper.

Place shallots, tarragon leaves, vinegar and peppercorns in small saucepan, cook on stove and reduce. Allow to cool. Add egg yolks and whisk continually on a bain-marie until a stiff consistency is obtained. Add melted butter, slowly whisking all the time. (Do not use the milk sediment at the bottom of the melted butter.) Season to taste. Strain through a fine sieve. Add chopped tarragon leaves. Serve warm for it will curdle if hot.

BOLOGNAISE SAUCE (serve with alimentary pastes, rice, steak, etc.)

4 oz. *finely chopped beef. Chopped parsley.* 2 *peeled and diced tomatoes.* 2 *chopped shallots.* 1 *clove chopped garlic.* 2 *tablespoons oil or fat.* ¼ *pint light-brown sauce. Seasoning of salt and pepper.*

Heat oil or fat in a saucepan, add meat and shallots, fry briskly for 2 or 3 minutes ; add garlic and tomatoes ; add light-brown sauce, season ; cook slowly for 1 hour. Add chopped parsley.

BORDELAISE SAUCE (excellent with fried steak)

Fry slowly ½ oz. butter and 1 oz. chopped shallots. When shallots are soft and brown, add 1 gill red Bordeaux wine, 5 crushed peppercorns, and a pinch of powdered thyme. Then boil for 5 minutes ; add ½ pint brown sauce, simmer for 15 minutes, strain and season to taste. (If you have a marrow bone, poach a few slices of the marrow in a little stock for 5 or 6 minutes and serve them as garnish for the steak.)

BREAD SAUCE (serve with roast chicken, roast patridge, roast pheasant, roast grouse, roast turkey)

1 *cup stale bread-crumbs.* ½ *pint milk.* ½ *oz. butter.* ½ *teaspoon salt.* 2 *cloves.* 1 *small onion.*

Simmer the onion stuck with cloves in the milk for 15 minutes, strain the milk over the bread-crumbs, add seasoning and butter, and re-heat.

CRANBERRY SAUCE (serve with roast turkey, roast game)

1 *small tin cranberries. Diluted cornflour.*

Bring cranberries to the boil, thicken with diluted cornflour, cook for 5 to 10 minutes.

CHAUDFROID SAUCE (used as a coating for cold white meats, poultry)

1 *oz. margarine.* 1 *oz. flour.* ½ *pint stock.* 2 *sheets gelatine (soak in cold water).* ¼ *pint cream. Seasoning of salt and pepper.*

Melt the margarine, add the flour, cook. (White roux.) Stir in stock, whisk well together until smooth. Cook for 45 minutes. Remove. Add the gelatine, mix well until dissolved. Strain. Allow to cool. Add cream and correct seasoning.

CROÛTONS (use in soups, etc.)

Remove crusts from finely sliced stale bread; spread finely with butter, then cut into small cubes and fry in deep fat.

DEVILLED SAUCE (serve with grilled chicken, white meats, hamburgers, also fish)

4 *chopped shallots.* ⅛ *pint brown sauce.* 16 *crushed peppercorns.* 2 *dessertspoons vinegar. A few tarragon stalks.*

Place shallots, peppercorns, tarragon stalks and vinegar in a saucepan. Simmer slowly until reduced to a glaze. Add brown sauce and cook for a further 5 minutes. Strain.

DUMPLINGS (serve with boiled beef)

Suet crust, rather moist.

Roll into balls. Cook tightly covered with meat for 20 to 30 minutes.

EGG AND BREAD-CRUMB (this is the procedure to carry out for all foods requiring bread-crumbing, i.e., fillets of fish, veal escallopes or cutlets, lamb cutlets, chicken cutlets, potato croquettes, etc.)

2 *oz. flour.* 1 *egg, beaten with a pinch of salt.*
2 *cups stale bread-crumbs.*

Dip in flour, shake through egg, drain slightly,
bread-crumb. Remove, pat or flatten with a
knife.

FRIED PARSLEY

Wash parsley and remove the stalks. Dry. Heat
fat in a pan until hot ("blue vapour"). Deep-
fry parsley. Drain. Season.

GRAVY (for roasts)

Pour fat from the tray carefully, retaining the
sediment and juice of meat, poultry or game.
Place the tray on the stove, re-boil and reduce
to a glaze. Add ½ cup stock or vegetable water
(quantity of stock varying according to size of
joint, poultry or game), cook slowly for 5 minutes ; season and strain. Serve separately.

THICK BROWN GRAVY (serve with stuffed meats)

Strain off nearly all the dripping or fat, retaining
just enough to blend with 1 dessertspoon flour ;
mix together and cook until brown. Gradually
add ½ cup stock or vegetable water and then boil
for 5 minutes. Season. Serve separately.

HOLLANDAISE SAUCE (The "aristocratic" sauce ! Primarily served with boiled salmon, but may be served with fish generally, eggs, asparagus, artichokes, cauliflower, broccoli, or seakale.)

12 *grains of crushed peppercorns.* 2 *egg yolks.*
4 *oz. melted butter.* 1 *tablespoon vinegar.* 4 *drops
lemon juice.* 2 *tablespoons cold water. Seasoning
of salt and cayenne pepper.*

Place crushed peppercorns in small saucepan with vinegar and cook until vinegar is reduced seven-eighths. Strain. Add egg yolks, cold water, then whip up in a bain-marie until a stiff consistency is obtained and all air bubbles have disappeared. Remove and add melted butter, slowly whisking all the time. (Do not use the milk sediment at the bottom of the melted butter.) Add lemon juice and season to taste.

Variations of Hollandaise sauce :—

Mousseline or Chantilly Sauce (serve with fish, asparagus, eggs)
With cream—slowly add ½ cup whipped cream.

Béarnaise Sauce—add 1 tablespoon tarragon vinegar, 1 oz. each finely chopped tarragon leaves.

With Sherry—add 2 tablespoons sherry before removing from fire.

HORSE-RADISH SAUCE (serve with roast beef, smoked trout, etc.)

4 tablespoons grated horse-radish. 1½ tablespoons vinegar. Seasoning of cayenne pepper. ½ teaspoon salt. ½ cup of cream.

Mix horse-radish, vinegar, salt and seasoning together, add cream beaten stiff.

MADEIRA or SHERRY SAUCE (perfect with fillet of beef or braised sweetbreads)

1 gill Madeira wine or sweet sherry. 1 gill stock. ½ pint brown sauce. ½ oz. butter.

Boil Madeira wine or sherry with stock until quantity is reduced by about half ; strain into this liquid the brown sauce, boil for 5 minutes, and add butter before serving.

MADÈRE SAUCE (serve with veal cutlet)

1 *carrot.* 1 *onion.* 1 *tablespoon flour.* 1 *glass Madeira wine.* 1 *tablespoon fat.* 1 *bouquet garni.* ⅓ *pint stock.* 1 *tiny piece of garlic.*

Cut in small dice carrots and onion; fry in fat until brown, add flour (brown roux). Cook for 15 minutes. Stir in stock. Stir well, add bouquet garni and garlic; simmer for 2 hours. Strain. Add Madeira.

MARYLAND SAUCE

Boil ½ pint chicken stock or milk in a saucepan; mix 2 oz. butter and 1 teaspoon flour; stir well into stock or milk and boil for 10 minutes. Add some grated horse-radish and a little cream.

MAYONNAISE (serve with grilled or boiled salmon, fish generally, salads)

1 *egg yolk.* 1 *teaspoon vinegar.* ⅛ *pint olive oil.* 3 *dashes lemon juice. Seasoning of salt, pepper and pinch of mustard.*

Beat together in a basin the yolk, lemon juice' vinegar and seasoning. Add oil slowly, beating continually until a stiff consistency is obtained.

MINT SAUCE (with roast lamb)

¼ *cup mint leaves, finely chopped.* ½ *cup vinegar.* 1 *tablespoon sugar.*

Put mint and sugar in sauceboat; heat the vinegar (do not boil); then pour the vinegar over mint and sugar.

MORNAY SAUCE (serve with fish)

2 *oz. butter.* ½ *pint boiling milk.* 1 *tablespoon flour. Grated cheese. Seasoning of salt and pepper.*

Put butter in a small pan, stir in flour slowly.
Add boiling milk; stir well for 15 minutes.
Remove from fire, add a little grated cheese
and season to taste. 1 yolk of egg may be added,
if desired.

NAPOLITAINE SAUCE (serve with alimentary pastes, steak, etc.)

*⅛ pint oil. 2 cloves chopped garlic. ½ bay-leaf.
6 peeled tomatoes, roughly chopped, or 1 tin of
tomatoes (in the case of tinned tomatoes, drain
and chop). 1 chopped onion. Seasoning of salt
and pepper.*

Place oil in a saucepan, heat, add chopped onion,
cook for 5 minutes without colouring; add garlic,
then tomatoes, seasoning and bay-leaf, and cook
very slowly until the tomato is nearly dry.

PEASE PUDDING (serve with boiled bacon, boiled pork, or other boiled meats)

*1 gill split peas. Seasoning of salt and pepper.
1 oz. flour or 1 egg yolk. ½ oz. margarine or dripping.*

Wash peas and soak overnight in cold water. Tie
loosely in a pudding cloth and boil for 1 hour;
turn into a basin and mash smooth or pass
through a sieve. Add flour or yolk and seasoning. Press mixture into a greased pudding basin
and steam for 1 hour. Turn out.

PIQUANTE SAUCE (serve with tongue or boiled beef)

*2 oz. chopped shallots. ½ oz. butter. 3 small sliced
gherkins. 1 tablespoon vinegar. ½ pint brown
sauce. Chopped parsley. Seasoning of salt and
pepper.*

Fry shallots in butter until soft and brown. Add vinegar and boil for a few minutes until it is reduced to about three-quarters of its original quantity ; then add brown sauce and simmer for 15 minutes. Just before serving, add sliced gherkins and a little chopped parsley, and season to taste.

REDCURRANT JELLY (serve with roast leg mutton, roast lamb, roast hare, jugged hare, roast heart)

6 *lb. fruit (redcurrants). Sugar.*

Place the fruit and the stalks in a pan and cook slowly until tender. Mash and strain through a jelly-bag. Allow 1¼ lb. sugar to every 1 pint juice. Add sugar to the juice and stir whilst bringing to boiling point. Boil rapidly for 1 minute. Skim if necessary and bottle quickly.

SALSA VERDE (the delicious accompaniment for boiled beef, calf's head, boiled chicken, pot au feu)

1 *tablespoon of each of the following, finely chopped :—*

Anchovies, capers, gherkins, parsley, capsicums, chives or spring onions, garlic (if desired).

Add to an equal amount in bulk of vinaigrette dressing. (See Salad Dressings, page 235).

SAUCE VERTE (serve with salmon trout, fish generally)

Blanched spinach, watercress, tarragon, parsley, passed through a fine sieve and mixed with mayonnaise.

SHRIMP SAUCE (serve with fish, eggs, etc.)

¼ pint shrimps, washed, skinned, picked. ½ pint fish stock. 1 oz. butter or margarine. 1 oz. flour. 1 dessertspoon anchovy essence. Seasoning of cayenne pepper.

Melt butter or margarine, gradually stir in flour and stock; bring to the boil, whisk well; add anchovy essence and shrimps; season.

SMITANE SAUCE

1 tablespoon butter. 2 tablespoons grated onion. 1 measure dry white wine. 1½ cups thick sour cream. Seasoning of salt and pepper.

Sauté onion in butter lightly until soft, stirring continually; moisten with white wine; stir in sour cream, stirring continually; bring to the boil, strain, and season.

TARTARE SAUCE

1 egg yolk. 1 teaspoon vinegar. 1 teaspoon each capers, parsley, tarragon, finely chopped. 1 tablespoon gherkins, finely chopped. Seasoning of salt, pepper and mustard. 3 drops of lemon juice. ⅛ pint oil.

This is a mayonnaise sauce. Beat together in a basin—yolk, seasoning, lemon juice, vinegar. Add slowly oil, beating continually. To this add capers, parsley, tarragon and gherkins.

TOMATO SAUCE (1) (serve with roast pork, roast duck, roast goose)

Place ripe tomatoes, sliced, in a saucepan, add a few bay-leaves and a pinch of salt; simmer till soft, continually stirring, then pass the mixture through a sieve and cast aside the remaining tomato peels and pips. Re-boil the syrup, stirring continually, until it thickens. (This may be preserved in bottle.)

TOMATO SAUCE (2) (serve with alimentary pastes, rice, steak)

1 lb. tomatoes, peeled. 1 small onion, cut in dice. ¼ lb. butter or margarine. Dash of spice. ½ teaspoon salt. 2 tablespoons tomato purée.

Cook onion in butter until golden ; add spice and salt ; stir in tomatoes and tomato purée, finish cooking slowly for 5 minutes.

TYROLIENNE SAUCE (serve with fish)

1 egg yolk. 1 gherkin. ⅛ pint oil. 2 anchovies. ½ tablespoon capers. 3 dashes lemon juice. ½ tablespoon parsley. 1 teaspoon vinegar. ½ tablespoon tarragon. 1 dessertspoon tomato ketchup or purée. Seasoning of salt, pepper and a pinch of mustard.

This is a mayonnaise sauce. Beat together in a basin the yolk, lemon juice, vinegar and seasoning. Add oil slowly, beating continually until a stiff consistency is obtained. Finely chop together capers, parsley, tarragon, gherkin, anchovies, and add to the mayonnaise with the tomato ketchup.

YORKSHIRE PUDDING (serve with roast beef, of course !)

4 oz. flour. 3 eggs. ½ pint milk. Seasoning of salt, pepper and grated nutmeg.

Mix all ingredients into a smooth paste. Cover bottom of frying-pan or roasting-pan with some beef fat fried out from roast, pour in the batter ½ inch deep, and place in a hot oven for 5 minutes, then reduce the oven temperature and continue baking for approximately **15** minutes. For serving, cut in squares. Serve very hot with the roast beef.

Notes :—

Bouquet garni. Thyme, ba-yleaf, parsley stalks, chervil, tarragon, celery, leek, tied together and added to sauces or stews for flavouring.

Glaze. To colour a sauce under the grill, or in a hot oven.

Reduce to a glaze. To reduce stock of meat of fish on full fire until there is practically nothing left. This concentrates all the flavour into a small quantity ; it can then be built with cream or butter, etc. (i.e., Bovril is a reduction of meat stock).

Storing a sauce. If you wish to keep left-over sauce or, alternatively, if you wish to prepare sauce in advance and store until needed, put in a narrow jar and cover with a fine layer of melted butter.

Vinegar. It is best to use wine vinegar in special sauces.

SAVOURY BUTTERS

Butter in these recipes should be rather soft.

ANCHOVY BUTTER (use for fish generally, also steak)

3 *tablespoons butter.* 4 *anchovies, crushed.*

Mix well both ingredients ; strain through tammycloth or sieve.

BEURRE NOIR (Black Butter) (use for eggs, certain fish like skate, brains, etc.)

2 *tablespoons butter.* 1 *teaspoon lemon juice. Seasoning of salt and pepper.*

Add butter to fat remaining in pan after frying fish or meat, stir until brown, add lemon juice and season.

BUTTER COLBERT (use for fish generally, and grills)

3 tablespoons butter. 1 tablespoon cold melted meat glaze. Chopped parsley. Chopped tarragon. 1 teaspoon lemon juice. Seasoning of salt, and pepper.

Mix butter and glaze, add parsley, tarragon, lemon juice, and season.

BUTTER BERCY (serve with grilled porterhouse steak)

½ cup white wine. 3 tablespoons beef marrow, cooked in water and diced. Seasoning of salt pepper and lemon juice. 2 chopped shallots. 2 tablespoons butter.

Reduce wine and shallots; add marrow and butter, then seasoning.

LOBSTER BUTTER (use for fish generally); (also to colour lobster)

½ cup butter. Lobster coral, sieved.

Pound butter and coral until blended.

MAÎTRE D'HÔTEL BUTTER (use for fish and grills generally)

3 tablespoons butter. 1 tablespoon lemon juice. Chopped parsley.

Cream butter with parsley and very gradually add lemon juice.

MUSTARD BUTTER (use for fish generally, etc.)

3 tablespoons butter. 1 tablespoon mustard. Seasoning of salt and pepper.

Mix well butter with other ingredients.

PARSLEY BUTTER (use for fish, meats, and for snails, periwinkles, etc., served "au naturel")

3 *tablespoons butter. Chopped parsley.*

Mix together.

SHRIMP BUTTER (use for fish generally)

3 *tablespoons butter.* 2 *oz. pink shrimps.*

Mix well both ingredients; strain through tammycloth or sieve.

SWEET SAUCES

APRICOT SAUCE

2 *tablespoons apricot jam.* 2 *tablespoons water.*

Bring to the boil, strain, serve very hot.

ABRICOTINE AU RHUM SAUCE

2 *tablespoons apricot jam.* 1 *measure of rum* 2 *tablespoons water.*

Bring to the boil, strain, serve very hot.

BRANDY BUTTER (perfect with Christmas pudding)

4 *oz. butter.* ½ *oz. castor sugar.* 1 *measure of brandy.*

Cream butter and sugar together, add brandy drop by drop, beat well. Keep cold.

BRANDY SAUCE

3 *egg yolks.* ½ *pint cream.* 1 *measure of brandy.* 1 *tablespoon castor sugar.*

Place yolks into double-pan, add brandy, cream and sugar; whisk until a stiff consistency is obtained.

CARAMEL SAUCE

1 *cup demerara sugar.* ½ *cup water.*

Boil until a light-brown colour ; then add ¾ cup of water and boil until of desired consistency.

CHOCOLATE SAUCE

½ *cup water.* 1 *cup sugar.* 2 *squares chocolate (melted over hot water),* or 3 *oz. cocoa. Few grains cream of tartar.* ¼ *teaspoon vanilla essence.*

Boil water, sugar and cream of tartar for 5 minutes. When ready, pour slowly on chocolate. Allow to cool slightly and flavour with vanilla essence. May be served hot or cold.

GINGER SAUCE

1 *oz. butter or margarine.* 1 *oz. flour.* ½ *pint milk.* 1 *oz. preserved ginger, chopped into small dice.* 1 *tablespoon preserved ginger syrup.*

Melt butter, stir in flour and milk, bring to the boil and whisk until a smooth consistency is obtained ; add syrup and chopped ginger ; re-heat.

JAM SAUCE

1 *cup loaf sugar.* 1 *dessertspoon jam.* ¼ *pint water.* ½ *tablespoon lemon juice.*

Melt sugar in the water, stir in the jam, boil for 10 minutes and add lemon juice.

LEMON SAUCE

1 *pint water.* 3 *oz. sugar. Rind and juice of* 2 *lemons.* 2 *teaspoons cornflour.*

Let simmer water and lemon rind for 10 minutes ; strain ; add cornflour, lemon juice and sugar ; stir and bring to the boil.

MARSHMALLOW SAUCE

½ *pint water.* ½ *lb. marshmallows.*

Place marshmallows in the water and melt by warming gradually.

MELBA SAUCE

1 *cup raspberries (tinned or fresh).* ¼ *cup sugar.*

Crush raspberries, add sugar, cook to a syrup. Strain.

RED SAUCE (use as fruit covering)

2 *tablespoons redcurrant jelly.* 2 *tablespoons water.*

Bring to the boil till dissolved and cover fruit with same.

STRAWBERRY PURÉE

2 *cups strawberries, washed and hulled.* 1 *cup sugar.*

Mash strawberries, add sugar and let stand for 1 hour.

SWEET WHITE SAUCE

1 *oz. butter or margarine.* ½ *oz. flour.* ½ *pint milk.* 1 *oz. castor sugar. Vanilla essence.*

Melt the butter, stir in the flour and the milk, continue stirring and bring to the boil ; add castor sugar and vanilla essence.

SABAYON SAUCE

1 *egg.* 1 *egg yolk.* 1 *measure sherry or rum.* 1 *tablespoon castor sugar.*

Put all into a basin and beat until stiff over a bowl of hot water.

STUFFINGS AND FORCEMEATS FOR POULTRY, MEAT AND FISH

CHESTNUT (for meats, poultry)

1 *lb. veal. 4 oz. fresh lard. 24 chestnuts. 2 oz. chopped parsley. 1 lb. soaked bread. Seasoning of salt, pepper, nutmeg, thyme. 2 eggs.*

Finely mince veal and lard. Add parsley, eggs, bread and seasoning. Split and half-roast the chestnuts, peel, add to the mixture. (For **turkey stuffing**—the turkey liver, finely chopped, may be added, if desired.)

CHICKEN (for poultry)

4 *oz. pork. 8 oz. chicken meat, raw. 8 oz. veal. 1 lb. fresh lard. 4 eggs. 1 measure brandy. Seasoning of salt, pepper, mixed spice, nutmeg.*

Pass through a mincer (first large then fine plates) first four items until a fine pulp is obtained. Add seasoning, eggs and brandy.

FOIE GRAS (for meats, poultry)

1 *egg. 4 oz. foie gras. 8 oz. chicken liver. 4 oz. butter. 1 measure sherry or brandy. Seasoning of salt, pepper, nutmeg, cayenne pepper.*

Finely chop liver, then work all ingredients into a mixture.

CELERY STUFFING

1 *cup bread-crumbs. ½ cup chopped celery. 1 tablespoon butter. 1 dessertspoon minced onion. 1 tablespoon chopped parsley. Seasoning of salt and pepper.*

Cook celery, onion and parsley in the butter for 3 or 4 minutes; then add bread-crumbs and seasoning.

CHICKEN, VEAL, FISH, QUENELLES (This may be used as a stuffing but is also a very light and nourishing dish shaped into small balls or round croquettes deep-fried or baked and served with tomato or mushroom sauce)

Make a panada with ¼ pint milk, 1 oz. butter, and 1 oz. flour. When milk and butter are boiling, add flour and stir well into a thick paste. (If paste not thick enough, add more flour.) Allow to cool.

Stuffing for quenelles : — 1 cup finely minced raw veal or chicken meat, or raw fish with firm flesh (pike is a good fish to select), seasoning of salt and pepper ; mix with panada, add 1 egg yolk (also 1 tablespoon whipped cream, if desired), and pass mixture through a sieve.

FISH, CHICKEN or VEAL FORCEMEAT

(fish forcemeat used for baked fish ; meat forcemeat for poultry ; both are suitable for vegetable stuffing)

1 *cup stale bread-crumbs. ½ cup milk. 1½ tablespoons butter or margarine. Seasoning of salt, nutmeg, and 3 drops Tabasco sauce. 1 cup finely minced raw veal or chicken meat, or raw fish, or cooked or tinned lobster, shrimp, or crab meat.*

Slowly cook bread-crumbs and milk in a saucepan ; stir to a paste. Add butter, seasoning, and meat or fish ; beat until a smooth mixture is obtained.

FORCEMEAT BALLS

2 *tablespoons bread-crumbs. 1 tablespoon suet. 1 tablespoon chopped parsley. Egg, beaten, for binding. Seasoning of salt and pepper. 1 teaspoon dried mixed herbs.*

Mix all dry ingredients together, then add enough egg to bind. Shape into small balls (with floured hands). These balls may be bread-crumbed and fried, or added to stews or casseroles 15 minutes before serving.

LIVER (for poultry)

1 *cup grated Parmesan cheese.* 1 *egg. Liver of poultry.* 1 *cup bread-crumbs. Seasoning of salt, spice, speck of garlic, parsley.*

Finely chop liver and seasoning together, mix with cheese and bread-crumbs, bind the whole mixture with egg.

ORDINARY SAUSAGE (for meats, poultry)

8 *oz. lean pork or beef.* 1 *lb. soaked bread.* 8 *oz. fresh lard. Seasoning of salt, pepper, mixed spice, nutmeg.*

Finely mince meat and lard, then work all ingredients into a sausage mixture.

OYSTER (for turkey or chicken)

$\frac{1}{4}$ *cup melted butter or margarine.* $\frac{1}{2}$ *cup chopped onion.* $\frac{1}{2}$ *cup diced celery.* 1 *pint fresh halved, drained, and coarsely chopped oysters (tough muscles removed).* $\frac{1}{2}$ *teaspoon Tabasco sauce or lemon juice.* 6 *cups bread-crumbs.* 2 *tablespoons chopped parsley.* $\frac{1}{2}$ *teaspoon salt and pepper.*

Add onion and celery to melted butter; cook until tender; add Tabasco sauce, bread-crumbs, chopped parsley, salt. Fry slowly for 5 minutes, stirring continually; add oysters.

PRUNE (for goose or duck)

$\frac{3}{4}$ *cup cooked prunes, pitted and chopped.* 1 *cup chopped walnuts or Brazil nuts.* 1 *dessertspoon onion, finely chopped.* 1 *egg.* 3 *cups bread-crumbs.*

2 *tablespoons melted butter or margarine.* ½ *tea-spoon salt.* ¼ *teaspoon pepper.* ½ *cup boiling water or prune syrup.*

Work all ingredients into a mixture. (Chopped and cooked goose giblets may be added, if desired.) As fruit swells, stuff goose or duck only two-thirds full.

SAGE AND ONION (for meats, poultry)

2 *large onions.* ½ *lb. bread-crumbs.* 1 *oz. sage. Chopped parsley.* 4 *oz. fat or dripping. Seasoning of salt and pepper.*

Finely chop the onions. Heat fat, add onions, cook slowly for 10 minutes. Add sage, mix well, stir in the bread-crumbs. Season. Cook in the oven for 20 minutes. If desired, a little gravy may be added. (If possible use dripping from joint or poultry for which the stuffing is required, i.e., pork fat, duck fat, goose fat, etc.)

VEAL (for meats, poultry)

4 *oz. veal.* 4 *oz. pork.* ½ *lb. fresh lard.* 2 *eggs.* 1 *measure brandy. Seasoning of salt, pepper, mixed spice, nutmeg.*

Pass through a mincer (first large then fine plates) first three items until a fine pulp is obtained. Add seasoning, eggs and brandy.

RICE

HOW TO WASH RICE

Put rice in strainer, then put strainer over basin-
ful of cold water; rub rice between your hands,
lift strainer from basin and change the water.
Repeat two or three times until water is clear.

RE-HEATED RICE

Rice left-overs may be added to boiling salted
water or milk or stock, cooked for 5 minutes,
drained and allowed to dry out.

Alternatively, rice left-overs may be re-heated in
the oven by adding a little water or milk or stock
to the pan, covering and cooking until grains
are well heated.

BAKED RICE

Place well-washed rice in earthenware dish, cover
well with salted water and bake in moderate oven
until rice is absorbed by water.

BOILED RICE (1)

Have water fast boiling, add 1 tablespoon salt to
every quart; wash rice in several waters and pick
out any husks or black pieces just before throw-
ing into boiling water; boil quickly for 8-10 minutes; drain and toss with a fork.

BOILED RICE (2)

Wash and pick over, say, 1 lb. rice, add to boiling
salted water slowly; boil for 20 minutes or until
there is no hard spot in centre. Drain. Return
to kettle in which it was cooked. Cover, let stand
in warm place to dry off, when each grain will be
separate. To stir rice, always use a fork to avoid
breaking kernels.

STEAMED RICE

1 *cup rice.* 1 *teaspoon salt.* 3 *cups boiling water.*

Put salt and water in top of double boiler, placed directly over heat and add gradually well-washed rice, stirring with fork to prevent sticking to boiler. Boil 5 minutes, cover, place over lower part of double boiler, and steam 45 minutes, or until kernels are soft; uncover so that steam may escape.

BROWN RICE or WILD RICE

Cooked in similar manner as white rice but cooking time twice as long. To shorten the cooking period, soften bran coats by soaking 1 hour in lukewarm water beforehand.

CURRY

1½ *lb. cooked veal, lamb or any meat or poultry remnants, cut into* 1½ *inch dice.* 1 *onion, sliced.* ½ *cup butter or any fat.* 1½ *tablespoons curry powder.* 1 *large cooking apple, peeled and diced (to mellow sharp flavour).* 2 *cups stock or water.* 1 *bay-leaf. Steamed rice. Seasoning of salt.*

Fry onion and apple in butter or fat in small saucepan; add meat, seasoning and bay-leaf; stir in curry; then stir in stock and let simmer for 20-30 minutes or until meat is tender. (If desired, 1 teaspoon lemon juice or vinegar may be added.) Serve with steamed rice. A variety of accompaniments may be served with curry, such as, sliced banana, grated coconut, chopped almonds. Pass round separately Bombay Ducks and puppodums (obtainable in big provision stores) and chutney.

RICE À LA CRÉOLE or À L'INDIENNE

1 large onion, thinly sliced. 2 green peppers, seeded and shredded. 4 tablespoons butter. 1 cup rice, well-washed and drained. 1 bouquet garni. ¼ lb. mushrooms, peeled and sliced. 3 tomatoes, peeled and chopped. ½ cup olives, pitted and sliced. Seasoning of salt and black pepper. 1 clove of garlic. 2 cups boiling water.

Cook gently onion and green peppers in butter for 5 minutes. Gradually stir in rice and continue stirring until rice is golden ; add mushrooms, tomatoes, olives, seasoning, bouquet garni, and garlic. Mix well, then stir in boiling water. Cover and let simmer for 45 minutes in a moderate oven. When ready, discard bouquet garni and serve from the casserole.

RICE PILAFF

1 chopped onion. 1 cup rice. 1 oz. butter or margarine. 1 bouquet garni. 2 cups stock or water. Seasoning of salt and pepper.

Pick the rice. Place onion and margarine in a pan, lightly fry without colouring, add rice and stir well. Pour in the stock. Season, add bouquet garni. Bring to the boil, cover, cook in a hot oven for 18 to 20 minutes. Remove, allow to settle for 5 minutes, throw away the bouquet garni. Break down the rice with a fork and add a little butter.

RICE PUDDING

There are one or two ways of making rice pudding but my favourite is my mother's simple yet tasty way :

1 lb. rice (serves 6). 2 eggs, well whisked. 1 teacup granulated sugar. 1½ pints milk.

Beat together milk, eggs, sugar; place well-washed rice in pie-dish, pour mixture over rice; bake in moderate oven for ¾ hour.
A cheaper way, of course, is to replace eggs with custard powder.

RISI-PISI

Make risotto—minus saffron—and add green peas stewed with butter. If desired, cover and serve with shrimp sauce.

RISOTTO À LA GRECQUE

Make a rice pilaff; add minced lettuce leaves, small dice of sweet pimento and ½ cup cooked green peas.

RISOTTO MILANAISE

1 lb. Italian rice (if not obtainable use Carolina rice). 2 pints beef or chicken stock or white consommé. 1 onion, chopped. Pinch of saffron. 4 oz. butter. 2 tablespoons grated Parmesan cheese. Seasoning of salt and pepper.

Fry in saucepan chopped onion in 3 oz. butter until golden brown. Add rice and saffron; mix well and fry over a quick fire for a couple of minutes, stirring all the time. Have ready on the side at boiling point stock or white consommé; add gradually to the rice in small quantities stirring continually. Season to taste. Cook from 18 to 20 minutes, stirring occasionally. Just before it is ready, add Parmesan cheese. When ready, remove from fire and stir in 1 oz. butter. (If desired, add chopped mushrooms, kidney or chicken liver cut in square pieces, or chopped meat, to the onion before rice is put in. Also half a glass of red or white wine before adding the stock). Risotto should be accompanied by a separate dish of grated Parmesan cheese.

Left-over risotto may be used again in the following manner :—

RISOTTO AL SALTO

2 *tablespoons butter. Left-over risotto.*

Melt butter in frying-pan until golden ; add left-over risotto ; stir frying-pan constantly for about half a minute and until flat omelette shape is obtained ; let cook one side until golden brown, then turn and cook other side. (A good old-fashioned method of turning is to place a plate over frying-pan, turn over, then slide "rice omelette" back into pan).

RICE FLAN

(This is a lovely sweet speciality from Belgium and a nice way of using up left-over boiled rice.)

Paste :

½ *lb. flour.* ¼ *lb. lard.* ½ *lb. sugar.* 1 *egg.* 1 *tablespoon of milk. Pinch of salt.*

Cream sugar and fat together, add egg, stir in the flour, milk and salt. Mix lightly together, allow to stand for ½ hour. Roll out and line a greased flan ring.

4 *oz. boiled rice.* 2 *eggs.* 1 *oz. sugar.* 1 *gill of milk. Dash of vanilla essence.*

Beat eggs, milk, sugar, vanilla essence together ; add rice, mix well. Pour into the flan ring and bake in a moderate oven for ½ hour. Allow to cool before cutting. The rice flan may be decorated with seasonal fruit, such as strawberries, raspberries, sliced peaches, etc.

ALIMENTARY PASTES

These recipes are economical to produce yet very nutritious and certainly they have a surprising appeal to children.

CANNELONI

1 *lb. flour.* 2 *eggs.* 1 *oz. butter. Seasoning of salt.*

Make into a paste. Roll out very thin. Cut into 4-inch squares. Poach squares for 2 minutes in boiling salted water. Drain. Place in cold water. When cold, dry with a cloth.

MIXTURE FOR STUFFING

8 oz. braised beef. 8 oz. cooked leaf spinach. 2 oz. shallots. 1 clove of garlic. 2 eggs. 4 oz. cooked calves' brains (if possible). Grated Parmesan cheese. Seasoning of salt, pepper and grated nutmeg.

Chop very finely, then mix all the ingredients together and season well. Spread mixture on the squares. Roll up. Place in buttered dish. Sprinkle with Parmesan cheese. Cook slowly in oven for 10 minutes. Surround with a hot light-brown sauce. Leave in oven for 5 minutes, serve very hot.

GNOCCHI ROMANA

1 pint of milk. ½ lb. semolina. 1 egg yolk. Cream. 1 oz. grated Parmesan cheese. Dabs of butter. Seasoning of salt, pepper and grated nutmeg.

Bring milk to the boil and season. Rain in semolina, stirring briskly all the time. When thick, cover tightly and cook on the stove for 20 minutes. Remove from the fire, beat in egg yolk and grated Parmesan cheese. Pour into a buttered tin. When cold, cut into round rings the size of a penny and ½ inch thick. Place in an earthenware dish, sprinkle with Parmesan cheese, surround with a little cream, add a few dabs of butter, and brown in the oven. Serve very hot.

GNOCCHI PIEMONTESE

3 lb. potatoes, peeled. ½ teaspoon salt. 1½ lb. plain flour.

Boil potatoes with salt, drain, and, while still hot, mix in with flour and blend thoroughly into a paste. Turn on to a floured board, shape into long sausage-like strips ½ inch thick, cut into balls the size of a walnut, then curl each "walnut" with fork or thumb. Poach the gnocchi in boiling salted water for about 35 to 40 minutes, drain, and serve immediately with tomato sauce (2) and grated Parmesan cheese.

FETTUCINE
TAGLIATELLE

(These are both noodle pastes but tagliatelle are slightly larger than fettucine.)

1 *lb. fettucine or tagliatelle.*

Drop into a large pan full of boiling salted water. Move with a fork occasionally. Cook for approximately 18 minutes. Drain thoroughly. Serve at once, topped with a few dabs of butter and sprinkled with grated Parmesan cheese. Alternatively, serve with Napolitaine sauce.

LASAGNE VERDE

(Green noodles—coloured green with spinach.)

1 *lb. lasagne verde.*

Cook in plenty of fast-boiling salted water. Move with a fork occasionally. Cook for approximately 18 minutes, leave a little on the firm side. Drain well. Place in a dish, add dabs of butter and grated Parmesan cheese. Toss lightly to obtain a creamy effect but do not re-heat in any way. Serve at once.

MACARONI

1 *lb. macaroni. Dabs of butter. Grated Parmesan cheese. Seasoning of salt.*

Boil broken macaroni in plenty of fast-boiling salted water for 25 to 30 minutes; stir with fork occasionally. Keep on the firm side. Do not over-cook. Drain very well. Place in a dish. Add dabs of butter and grated Parmesan cheese; toss and mix well together; season. Serve at once. Bolognaise sauce, Napolitaine sauce or 2 cups cream sauce may be added. (Latter is fattening but who cares when it is such a lovely dish!) Grated Parmesan cheese served separately.

SPAGHETTI

1 *lb. spaghetti. Dabs of butter. Grated Parmesan cheese. Seasoning of salt.*

Boil spaghetti in plenty of fast-boiling salted water for 18 to 20 minutes; stir with a fork occasionally. Keep on the firm side, do not over-cook. (Italians prefer to cook them for only 10 to 12 minutes because they like them "al dente" or, as we say, hard.) Drain very well. Place in a dish. Add dabs of butter and grated Parmesan cheese; toss and mix well together; season. Serve at once.
Bolognaise sauce or Napolitaine sauce may be added. Grated Parmesan cheese served separately.

MACARONI ⎫ Left-overs may be used as
SPAGHETTI ⎭   follows : —

AU GRATIN

Covered with white sauce, topped with bread-crumbs, grated cheese and tiny knobs of butter; browned quickly under the grill or in a hot oven.

TIMBALES

Line bottom and sides of buttered small moulds with left-over macaroni or spaghetti, fill with chicken or fish forcemeat (see page 180) two-thirds full, place in pan of hot water and bake in a moderate oven for 15 minutes or until firm. Let stand for 5 minutes before turning out of moulds, and serve with Hollandaise or Béchamel sauce.

MANICOTTI ALLA TOSCANA

(A dish from romantic Tuscany which is rarely tasted here but is delicious and, if tried once, will be made again for sure. In Italy, goat's cream cheese is used instead of sour milk so, to those who reside in the country and perhaps stand more chance of obtaining goat's cream cheese than the city-dwellers, go ahead and use it.)

Paste preparation :

1 *lb. flour.* 1 *oz. butter.* 2 *eggs. Seasoning of salt.*

Make into a paste and roll out very thin. Cut into 4-inch squares. Poach squares for 2 minutes in boiling salted water. Drain. Place in cold water. When cold, dry with a cloth. Spread flat on table.

MIXTURE FOR STUFFING

½ *pint sour milk or cream.* 4 *oz. chopped ham. Seasoning of salt, pepper, cayenne pepper.*

Mix all ingredients together. Spread mixture on the squares. Roll up. Place in buttered dish, sprinkle with grated Parmesan cheese, surround with a little cream, and cook slowly in oven until lightly brown. Serve at once.

POLENTA

1 *pint well salted fast-boiling water.* ½ *lb. yellow corn meal or maize semolina.*

Sprinkle into boiling water yellow corn meal and boil steadily on a slow fire, stirring continually with a wooden spoon to avoid lumping; cook until mixture cleanly leaves spoon. Turn on to dish. Then cut into slices. May be served plain with braised beef or stew, or with dabs of butter and grated Parmesan cheese.

Alternatively, after slicing, serve with Bolognaise sauce or Napolitaine sauce.

With left-over polenta make :

POLENTA PASTICCIATA

Cut left-over polenta into very thin slices, layer bottom of buttered baking-tin with slices, cover with Napolitaine sauce (with added sliced mushrooms and 1 tablespoon cream) and grated Parmesan cheese. Follow the same procedure three or four times and ensure top layer is sprinkled with grated Parmesan cheese and a few small knobs of butter. Bake in a moderate oven until golden-brown. Serve cut into slices.

RAVIOLI

(These are stuffed paste "pin-cushions".)

MIXTURE FOR STUFFING

5 oz. braised beef, or left-over cooked meat or poultry. ½ lb. spinach purée. Butter. 1 raw egg yolk. 1 crushed hard-boiled egg yolk. Seasoning of salt, pepper, nutmeg. 2 oz. grated dry Gruyère cheese.

Hash braised beef, mix with spinach well dried in butter, egg yolks, seasoning, and grated cheese.

Paste preparation :

½ lb. flour. 2 eggs. 1 teaspoon salt.

Pour flour into a mound on a large pastry-board, make a well in the middle and break in eggs, add salt. Fold flour over eggs and knead well with hands until mixture forms into a ball. Continue kneading for 10 minutes. Then roll out

paste into a very thin large square. Halve. Place
1 teaspoon of stuffing 1 inch apart until one
square is complete. Cover with second square.
Shape with cutter or egg-cup and press with
fingers around the shapes. Boil the ravioli in
fast-boiling salted water for approximately 20
minutes. Drain. Place in a dish, add dabs of
butter and sprinkle with grated Parmesan cheese.
Alternatively, serve with tomato sauce (2) or
Napolitaine Sauce, and grated Parmesan cheese
passed round separately.

Here are ways of using alimentary pastes in
soups :

CONSOMMÉ AUX CHEVEUX D'ANGE

(Vermicelli Consommé.)

1½ *quarts beef consommé.* ½ *lb. very small vermicelli.*

Bring to the boil consommé, drop in vermicelli
and cook for 5 minutes.

MACARONI or SPAGHETTI SOUP

1 *cup broken macaroni or spaghetti.* 5 *cups brown
stock or consommé stock.*

Bring to the boil stock, drop in paste and cook
for 5 minutes.
Note. —Left-over macaroni or spaghetti may
be added to soup and re-heated.

MINESTRONE

(In Italy, this soup is made so thick that, if the
soup-spoon is "stood" in the bowl, it will not
fall down. Here, instead, although it is rarely
made as thick, exists the common fault that only
the stock should be drunk and all the vegetables
should be left in the soup-plate !)

2 lb. of all kinds of vegetables, according to the season. 1 lb. shin beef and a knuckle-bone (chopped by the butcher). 3 pints salted water. 1 clove of garlic. 1 dessertspoon chopped parsley. ½ lb. broken spaghetti (or vermicelli), or pastine or any of the small-shaped pasta, such as little shells, little stars, and so on. (Rice may replace pasta.) 2 leeks or onions. Grated Parmesan cheese.

Place beef and knuckle-bone in salted water, with leeks and garlic to give flavour. Bring to the boil, and simmer for 2 hours. Skim. Drain. Have prepared vegetables, such as skinned tomatoes, finely-shredded cabbage, shelled peas, diced carrots, haricot beans, diced celery, finely-cut runner beans, broad beans, diced potatoes, diced turnips, diced swedes ; place in the stock, re-boil and let simmer. When the vegetables are almost tender, add pasta or rice. Finish cooking for 10 minutes. Before serving, add chopped parsley. Serve in heated soup-plates or bowls, and pass a dish of grated Parmesan cheese on the side.

RAVIOLI SOUP

3 pints chicken or beef stock. ½ lb. ravioli. Grated Parmesan cheese.

Boil ravioli for 20 minutes in the stock. Add grated cheese and serve.

PASTRIES

TO FOLD OR CUT—means cutting
mixture with a knife, and
turning it over completely, lifting
it up from the bottom and sides
of the bowl, folding in
lightly till blended.

TO CREAM BUTTER OR MARGARINE
—place in warm bowl or basin
and beat lightly to-and-fro with
a wooden spoon until fluffy.

TO ADD EGGS—break eggs
separately into a cup, and then—
continually beating—drop one by
one into creamed fat and sugar.

SHAPING AND ROLLING OF PASTRY.
—Sprinkle flour on to pastry
board, turn in the edges lightly
until smooth ; then (with
rolling-pin) roll lightly in short
quick rolls to approximate
thickness desired.

*Cold water for mixing should
be* VERY *cold.
Rub in fat with fingertips.
Mix pastry speedily and lightly.
It is said that baking pastry—if
good—greases its own tin !
A rich cake needs a slow oven.
Pierce a cake in the middle
with a steel needle and, if it
comes out clean, it is cooked !*

ALMOND PASTRY

(Use for fruit tarts or pies.)

½ lb. sifted flour. ½ teaspoon salt. 5 oz. lard or other shortening. ¼ cup chopped blanched almonds. 3 tablespoons cold water.

Sift together flour and salt and rub in shortening ; stir in almonds, add enough water to make a dough. Roll out on to floured board and cut into required rounds or shapes. Bake in hot oven for approximately 10 minutes.

CHEESE PASTRY

(For cheese straws.)

2 oz. butter or margarine. 4 oz. sifted flour. 2 oz. grated Parmesan cheese. 1 oz. grated Cheddar cheese. 1 egg yolk. Salt and cayenne pepper. 1 tablespoon cold water.

Put flour and salt into a basin, rub in the fat ; add cayenne pepper and grated cheeses. Mix to a dough with egg yolk and water. Roll out to ¼-inch thickness. Turn into 3-inch wide strips. Cut into ¼-inch lengths for straws. Bake on a baking-sheet in a moderate oven for approximately 10 minutes.

CHOUX PASTRY (use for cases with savoury fillings, or for éclairs, cream buns, etc.)

½ pint water. 4 oz. flour. 4 oz. butter or margarine. 3 eggs. ¼ teaspoon salt.

Heat water and butter in a small saucepan until fat melts, add flour and salt ; stir continually and cook over low heat until mixture leaves sides of the pan. Allow to cool, then add eggs—thoroughly beating each one in separately yet keeping mixture nice and stiff.

For éclairs and cream buns :—

Force through a bag on to baking-sheet in respective shapes, then bake 25 to 30 minutes in moderate oven.

DOUGHNUT PASTRY

8 oz. flour. 2 oz. butter or margarine. 2 oz. castor sugar. ¼ teaspoon salt. 1 teaspoon baking powder. Milk.

Rub butter into flour, add other ingredients and mix to light paste with milk. Roll out ½ inch thick, cut into rings, then deep-fry in very hot fat. When ready, remove and sprinkle with castor sugar.

DUTCH PASTRY or ROUGH PUFF PASTRY
(use for sausage rolls, meat or mince pies, apple bande, etc.)

½ lb. flour (DO NOT USE SELF-RAISING FLOUR). *¼ pint water. ¼ teaspoon salt. 6 oz. butter or margarine. ½ teaspoon cream of tartar.*

Sieve flour, salt, cream of tartar, rub in the butter, mix to a dough, stand for 10 minutes. Roll out, fold in 3, turn, roll out again, stand for 5 minutes. Repeat once more. Stand for 10 minutes.

FLAKY PASTRY (use for savouries, sausage rolls, meat pies, etc.)

1 lb. flour (DO NOT USE SELF-RAISING FLOUR). *1 lb. lard or margarine. ¼ teaspoon salt. 1 dessertspoon lemon juice. Cold water.*

Sift flour and salt into a basin. Rub 5 oz. fat well chilled into flour and salt ; add lemon juice and enough water to make an elastic dough. Turn out on to floured board and work until smooth. Roll out to an oblong strip. Divide remainder of fat into three parts ; cut one-third into small lumps and spread on the pastry. Fold in 3, and roll out. Stand for 10 minutes. Repeat folding and rolling 4 times. Stand for 10 minutes at least before using.

FLAN PASTRY (use for flan and tartelette shells and such shells, if kept in airtight tin, can be used on any occasion and filled, as desired, with soft fruit, syrup, curd or jam)

Paste : —

2 *eggs.* $\frac{1}{2}$ *lb. flour.* $\frac{1}{2}$ *oz. baking-powder.* 2 *oz. sugar.* 2 *oz. lard.* 2 *oz. margarine.* $\frac{1}{4}$ *teaspoon salt.*

Cream sugar and fats together, add eggs, stir in the flour, salt and baking-powder. Mix lightly together, allow to stand $\frac{1}{2}$ hour. Roll out and line tartelette moulds. Bake in a moderate oven for 10 to 15 minutes. Remove. (For that extra touch—spread each tart-case a little prepared egg custard before filling.)

GENOESE PASTRY (use for pastry slice, fancy cakes, swiss rolls, etc.)

3 *eggs.* 3 *oz. melted butter or margarine.* 3 *oz. sifted flour.* 4 *oz. castor sugar.* $\frac{1}{4}$ *teaspoon salt.*

Put eggs and sugar into a bowl and stand over a large basin of hot water. Whisk until mixture is light and creamy ; add melted (lukewarm) butter ; delicately fold in the flour sifted with salt. Spread and shape accordingly, and bake in a hot oven for 5 to 10 minutes.

For Swiss Roll :—Spread mixture in a Swiss roll tin lined with greaseproof paper and bake in a hot oven for 5 minutes. Turn out on to sugared paper (remove greaseproof paper). Spread immediately with hot jam or desired filling. Cut off any crisp edges and roll up securely.

NEAPOLITAN PASTRY or PASTA "FROLLA" (this is an Italian shortbread; use for flan, tartelettes, etc.)

$\frac{1}{2}$ *lb. flour.* $\frac{1}{4}$ *cup crushed almonds.* 4 *oz. butter.* 5 *oz. castor sugar.* 2 *eggs.* $\frac{1}{4}$ *teaspoon salt.* 1 *teaspoon lemon or orange juice.*

Gradually add sugar to crushed almonds; add 1 egg; rub this mixture into the flour, then add butter, second egg, salt and lemon juice. Mix into a firm paste, then roll out. Stand for 1 hour before using.

POTATO PASTRY (use for tarts, etc.)

$\frac{1}{4}$ *lb. flour.* $\frac{1}{4}$ *lb. mashed potatoes.* 1 *teaspoon baking-powder.* $\frac{1}{4}$ *teaspoon salt.* 3 *oz. butter or margarine. Cold water.*

Sift flour, salt and baking-powder into a bowl, rub in the butter, add mashed potatoes and mix to a stiff paste with cold water. (If desired, a little cold milk may be added.) Roll out thinly before shaping accordingly.

PUFF PASTRY (use for vol-au-vent cases, meat or mincemeat pies, patties, puffs, etc.)

1 *lb. flour* (DO NOT USE SELF-RAISING FLOUR). 1 *lb. butter or margarine* (BUTTER IS BEST TO OBTAIN A GOOD PUFF-PASTE). 1 *teaspoon salt.* $\frac{1}{4}$ *pint water.*

Mix flour, salt and water to a paste. Stand for 10 minutes. Roll out into a circle, place butter inside, cover with paste. Turn over. Roll out oblong, fold in 3, turn round, roll out again, fold. Repeat this process twice, giving 10 minutes rest between each roll.

SHORT PASTRY (1) (use for fruit, jam, or custard tarts and flans, etc.)

¾ lb. flour. ½ lb. butter or margarine. ¼ lb. sugar. 2 egg yolks. ¼ teaspoon salt. ½ grated lemon peel (or a few drops vanilla essence).

Rub fat into flour, salt and lemon peel; add egg yolks and sugar to make a stiff paste. Let stand for ½ hour. Roll out and line moulds Bake in moderate oven for 10 to 15 minutes

For LEMON MERINGUE PIE

Short pastry or flan pastry, in flan case. Meringue. 3 eggs (use whites for the meringue). 2 lemons. ½ pint milk. ½ lb. castor sugar. 3 oz. flour. 1 dab of butter or margarine.

Bake the flan case. Allow to cool. Mix sugar with the flour, add milk gradually and mix to a smooth paste; add juice and grated rind of lemons; bring to the boil, stirring continually. Add butter and slowly stir in egg yolks. Allow to cool. Then pour into flan case. Heap meringue on top of pie, set in the oven.

For MERINGUE (for puddings, desserts, pies, etc.)

3 egg whites. 6 oz. castor sugar. ½ teaspoon vanilla essence.

Whisk egg whites until stiff, gradually add sugar and vanilla essence. Force through a bag on to greased baking-sheet in shapes and bake for 15 minutes in a warm oven. Serve as cakes or pile or heap on to pies, desserts, etc., then set in the oven.

SHORT PASTRY (2) (use for Cornish pasties, etc.)

¾ lb. flour. 4 oz. lard or shortening. 4 oz. butter or margarine. ¼ teaspoon salt. Cold water.

Rub fat into flour and salt ; add enough water to make a stiff paste. Roll out, shape accordingly, bake in a moderate oven for ½ hour.

SPONGE (use for cakes, trifles, sweet desserts)

4 eggs. 4 oz. castor sugar. 3 oz. sifted flour. ¼ teaspoon salt.

Place eggs and castor sugar in a bowl and whisk over a pan of hot water until a stiff consistency is obtained. Remove, and whisk until cold ; fold in flour and salt. Pour mixture into greased deep pan. (Mixture should reach only half-way.) Bake for about 1 hour in moderately slow oven to allow for steady rising. Turn out when almost cold.

SUET PASTE (use for meat or fruit puddings, dumplings, etc.)

½ lb. flour. ¼ teaspoon salt. 4 oz. suet. Cold water.

Put flour and salt in a bowl ; grate in suet ; add enough cold water to make a stiff dough ; roll out suet crust thinly before shaping for cooking.

For FRUIT PUDDING

Suet paste. Any fresh fruit, prepared and sliced if necessary. Sugar. 3 tablespoons water.

Roll out suet crust thinly and line a greased pudding basin with it ; fill basin with fruit, add sugar according to sweetness desired, and cold water. Cover with suet crust, seal the edges. Cover with pudding cloth and steam for approximately 2 hours.

For ROLY POLY

Suet paste. Jam.

Roll out paste thinly and spread with jam; roll up, seal edges, and tie in pudding cloth. Boil slowly for $1\frac{1}{2}$ to 2 hours.

TWO-CRUST PIE (suitable for fruit pie, pumpkin pie, etc.)

Flaky pastry. Short pastry.

Roll out paste $\frac{1}{8}$ inch thick. Divide into 2, allowing more paste for upper-crust. Roll each into circles slightly larger than pie-plate to allow for shrinking.

Fit under-crust to *ungreased* pie-plate, fill as desired, moisten edges lightly and cover with upper-crust; press edges firmly together. Prick upper-crust so as to let steam escape.

Any left-over cake may be used in the following way :—

TRIFLE

Layer a bowl with slices of cake, moisten well with sweet sherry, pour in some freshly made custard. Repeat this procedure. Finish or garnish with tinned fruit. Decorate with thick cream. Allow to set in a cool place.

And here is a way of making use of cake crumbs :—

OLD PLANTATION TARTS

2 *lb. golden syrup.* 4 *oz. cake crumbs.* 4 *oz. sultanas*
2 *oz. lemon curd.*

Warm syrup and mix with remaining ingredients ;
fill into patty pans lined with short pastry and
place a small paste ring on each. Bake in a
moderate oven.

With stale bread make a children's favourite :—

BREAD AND BUTTER PUDDING

6 *thin slices of stale bread, crusts removed, and
halved.* 1 *pint milk.* 1 *cup currants and raisins.*
2 *eggs, beaten.* 2 *tablespoons sugar.*

Layer a greased pie-dish with bread and sprinkle
each layer with currants and raisins. Add sugar
and milk to beaten eggs and pour over the bread.
Allow to stand for 10 minutes, then bake in a
moderate oven for 30 minutes.

*With "left-over" milk you can make the follow-
ing recipes :—*

CREAM CHEESE

Sour milk turns easily into a cream cheese—tie it
in a muslin-cloth and hang for a day.

DOUGHNUTS (made with sour milk)

1 *cup sugar.* 2 *eggs, beaten.* 1 *cup sour milk.*
2 *tablespoons melted butter. Flour.* 1 *teaspoon
salt.* 1 *teaspoon baking-powder.* $\frac{1}{2}$ *teaspoon grated
nutmeg.*

Mix all ingredients together ; place one-half of
mixture on floured board, knead, and roll out
$\frac{1}{4}$ inch thick. Shape with doughnut-cutter, fry

in deep hot fat, take up on a skewer, drain on brown paper. Add trimmings to remaining mixture, roll, shape, and fry as before. When cool, coat doughnuts with castor sugar.

PETITS-FOURS (Friandises)

These dainty sweetmeats, generally served with sweet, dessert or coffee, appeal to people of all ages with a "sweet tooth." There are numerous petits-fours but the ones given below are among the simplest, easily made at home, yet bound to be a success because of their originality, delight to the eye, and pleasure to the taste.

CAPRICES

3 oz. crushed almonds. 3 oz. powdered sugar. ½ oz. melted butter. 1 whole egg. 1 tablespoon thick cream. 1 tablespoon kirsch.

Mix almonds with sugar, beat in the egg, cream, melted butter, and kirsch until a soft paste is obtained. Fill small plaited paper squares with the mixture, top each with candied cherry, and bake in a moderate oven for 5 or 6 minutes. Serve in the paper squares.

CHOCOLATE OR COFFEE FUDGE

1 lb. powdered sugar. 1 oz. butter or margarine. ½ pint condensed milk. ½ teaspoon vanilla essence. 3 tablespoons chocolate or cocoa powder, or 1 dessertspoon coffee essence.

Brush shallow tin with melted butter; put condensed milk and sugar in a pan and boil, stirring continually; remove from fire, add vanilla essence and chocolate powder (or coffee essence) and beat with a wooden spoon until a thick consistency is obtained. Pour the mixture into the prepared tin immediately. When cold, cut into small squares.

GENOESE FORTUNES

Genoese pastry.

Roll out and cut pastry into various small shapes, stuff centres with jam or sweet butter cream (see Brandy Butter, page 176, and for chocolate butter substitute brandy with chocolate, and so on). Bake in a moderate oven.

LANGUES DE CHAT

2 oz. butter. 2 oz. powdered sugar. 2 oz. sifted flour. 2 egg whites. ½ teaspoon vanilla essence.

Cream butter with sugar and vanilla essence, whisk in egg whites. Blend in the flour. Force mixture through a forcing-bag on to floured baking-sheet in "small finger" sized shapes. Bake in a very hot oven for 5 minutes, then remove immediately.

MANDARIN CARAMEL

Mandarin slices dipped in hot caramel sauce and allowed to set.
White grapes, orange slices, stoned cherries also may be dipped in hot caramel sauce.

MERINGUE PETITS-FOURS

Meringue mixture.

Arrange meringue mixture into small shell shapes and bake. When ready, fill half the amount of shells with desired sweet butter cream and cover with remaining half.

NOUGAT

½ lb. *powdered sugar.* ½ lb. *chopped almonds (passed through a sieve).* 1 *teaspoon lemon juice.*

Melt sugar in a copper pan on the stove until caramelized; add lemon juice and chopped almonds. Remove from stove, pour mixture on to an *oiled* baking-sheet (to allow for easy removal). When required, cut into small squares. If desired, nougat may be dipped and covered in hot chocolate.

PEPPERMINT DROPS

¾ lb. *of icing sugar.* 2 *eggs.* 25 *drops of peppermint essence.*

Put all ingredients in a bowl and mix until a dough-like consistency is obtained, dry enough to clean the bowl. (If mixture is not dry enough, add more sugar.) Turn mixture on to a board and knead until all stickiness disappears. Roll into a thin even paste, using castor sugar to prevent it sticking to the rolling-pin. Cut into small rounds and place on a dish. Leave until the sweets become crisp and dry.

VISTARINOS

¼ lb. *crushed almonds.* ¼ lb. *powdered sugar.* ½ *teaspoon vanilla essence.* 2 *egg whites.* ½ *measure of sweet Italian liqueur. Candied fruit (well sugared).*

Gradually add sugar to crushed almonds, then egg whites, vanilla essence and sweet liqueur, until a soft mixture is obtained. Shape mixture into small crowns with a forcing-bag on to sheet of greaseproof paper and decorate crown centres with any candied fruit desired. Bake in a moderate oven for 6 minutes. Remove, brush them over with well sugared milk.

Note.—Powdered sugar is crushed castor or loaf sugar.

EGGS

One way of finding out whether an egg is fresh is to drop it into a basin of cold water ; a good egg sinks—a bad egg floats on the top. And when you break a fresh egg, the white is nice and thick and the yolk stands up above it firmly ; whereas, when you break a stale egg, the white is runny and the yolk tends to flatten out.

TO BOIL. Boil enough water to cover egg, put in egg, and let simmer gently ; if lightly boiled, for 3 minutes ; if hard boiled, for 8 to 10 minutes.

TO FRY. Melt a little fat in frying-pan ; break eggs into a cup, then slip into pan. Cook gently until egg is set. Lift with slice.

TO POACH. To poach an egg in the professional manner, to obtain a white ball with no yolk showing, add 2 tablespoons vinegar and ½ teaspoon salt to 1 pint water, bring to the boil, break each egg carefully into a cup separately, quickly yet gently slip each egg into boiling water and cook for 2½ minutes ; remove carefully, plunge into ordinary hot water to remove vinegar flavour and dry lightly on a cloth before serving.

TO SCRAMBLE. Beat equal quantity of eggs and milk, add seasoning of salt and pepper, melt butter or margarine in a saucepan, pour in egg mixture, heat, and stir well. Usually served on toast.

CHEESE SOUFFLÉ (a savoury)

3 eggs. ⅔ cup cream. 1 cup cheese, cut in small dice. ½ cup grated Parmesan cheese. Seasoning of salt, pepper, few grains cayenne, few gratings nutmeg.

Add egg yolks to cream and beat slightly, add cheese and seasoning. Whip egg whites stiffly and fold into mixture. Pour mixture into greased soufflé dish ⅔ full, and bake for 15 minutes in a hot oven or until soufflé rises well above the mould. SERVE AT ONCE !

STREGA SOUFFLÉ (Superb sweet dessert which is a great favourite of mine because the *strega* liqueur—owing to the special herbs used in its preparation—gives the soufflé a strong distinctive flavour and a beautiful bouquet)

1 *oz. butter or margarine ;* 1 *oz. flour ;* 1 *oz. sugar (mixed to a paste).* 1 *gill of milk.* 4 *eggs.* 1 *measure strega liqueur.*

Boil milk, add strega ; add paste, mix until smooth. Cook in a double-pan for 5 minutes. Add egg yolks, one at a time. Remove. Beat the whites into a stiff froth in a perfectly clean basin. Add a small portion of white to the soufflé mixture and beat thoroughly. Fold in the remainder of the white carefully. Place in greased and sugared mould and cook in a hot oven (turning the mould occasionally and carefully) for 20 to 30 minutes until the soufflé rises well above the mould.

SERVE AT ONCE ! Remember that a soufflé waits for no one !

Note.—Strega, which is popular as an after-dinner liqueur, is also ideal in other sweet desserts, such as, with strawberries, sliced oranges, trifle, fruit salad, etc.

EGGS BENEDICTINE

Use 1 crumpet for each egg. Place slice of ham on very hot crumpet, top with poached egg, cover with Hollandaise sauce. If available, add 2 slices of truffles, and serve very hot.

EGG EN COCOTTE ROSSINI (serves 4)

4 eggs. 4 slices of foie gras. Brown sauce. Seasoning of salt and pepper.

Grease cocotte with butter, place 1 slice of foie gras in each egg cocotte, break in each egg, season and bain-marie in the oven for 6 to 7 minutes. Add a ring of brown sauce before serving. Eggs should be creamy.

EGG EN GELÉE (serves 4)

8 eggs, lightly poached. 1 tin mousse de foie gras. Tarragon leaves. Aspic.

Prepare aspic by dissolving 1 leaf of gelatine in ½ pint stock. Season. (Several aspic jellies may be purchased ready-made and only require diluting in water.) Place a little foie gras in 8 egg cocottes, cover with aspic and stand until set. Place a poached egg on top of each, then fill the cocottes with aspic. Garnish with blanched tarragon leaves and allow to set. Serve very cold.

EGGS SUR LE PLAT

Melt a little butter in round-eared egg-dish, break in 2 eggs side by side, and place under the grill to solidify top of egg white. Season, and garnish with chopped parsley.

GULLS' EGGS

(Allow 2 eggs per person.) Make sure that eggs are fresh by pricking each one with a pin. Hard-boil. Serve in shell, accompanied with oriental salt. (If oriental salt is not available, mix equal quantities of cayenne pepper and salt together.)

Note.—Gulls' and plovers' eggs are in season May and June.

OMELETTE NATURE

2 *eggs. Seasoning of salt and pepper.* ½ *oz. butter.*

Place eggs in a basin, beat, add seasoning. Melt butter in an omelette-pan—should be hot—pour in egg mixture, stir, and as it sets lift it up and allow liquid part to flow to bottom. Double omelette over and slip on to a hot dish. Generally, omelette is served soft in the middle.

Now, with an omelette you can let your imagination run riot! You can fill an omelette nature with cooked tomatœs, cooked asparagus tips, left-over cooked chicken livers diced, left-over cooked kidneys diced, left-over cooked meat diced, cooked flaked fish, cooked mushrooms, or grated cheese.
On the other hand, you can cover an omellete with Mornay sauce, sprinkle with grated cheese, and glaze it under the grill before serving.

Further omelette variations :—

OMELETTE ESPAGNOLE (serves 4)

8 *eggs.* 1 *large tomato, skinned and chopped. Chopped chives.* 3 *small new potatoes, boiled and diced. Chopped parsley. Sliced pimentos. Fried onion rings.* 1 *tablespoon sliced onion, sauté.*

Mix in the beaten eggs with potatoes, tomato, parsley, chives, pimentos, onion, and place into a very hot, greased omelette-pan. Mix lightly until set, place under the grill to finish, turn out flat on a serving-dish and garnish with very hot fried onion rings. To serve, cut in 4 portions.

OMELETTE FINES HERBES

Mix in a variety of herbs, chopped together (such as chopped chives, tarragon, parsley, basil, chervil) with an ordinary omelette.

Sweet omelettes :—

OMELETTE AU RHUM

Sprinkle an omelette nature with sugar, cover with rum and set alight.

OMELETTE À LA CONFITURE

6 *eggs.* 1 *oz. castor sugar.* 2 *tablespoons of any jam.* 1 *pinch of salt.*

Beat eggs and salt together. Make the omelette and place jam in the centre before rolling up. Turn out on a dish and sprinkle with sugar. Brand with a red-hot poker, if available.

ORDINARY PANCAKES

½ *lb. flour.* 1¼ *pints milk.* 1 *oz. sugar. Lemon juice.* 3 *eggs. Pinch of salt.*

Sift flour, add salt and sugar. Beat eggs with 1 pint milk. Add flour and beat until smooth. Leave for as long as possible, preferably overnight, then add remainder of milk. Use red-hot frying-pan, minimum amount of fat, pour mixture into pan as thin as possible, turn over by tossing in the traditional manner until golden. Serve very hot with sprinkling of sugar and lemon.

If desired, mix grated orange peel with sugar, then sift over the pancakes.

CRÊPE NORMANDE

2 *oz. flour ;* 1 *egg ;* ⅓ *pint milk ; pinch of salt ;* ¼ *oz. sugar (mix into a batter).* 2 *cooking apples.* 1 *pinch of cinnamon.*

Rest batter as long as possible before use. Peel and finely slice apples and stew them with sugar. Have frying-pan red-hot brushed with a little butter, add batter very thinly, cook for 2 or 3 seconds, spread the pancake with apples ; cover the apples with more batter, then turn pancake over and cook the other side. Serve flat and very hot with a sprinkling of sugar and cinnamon. It certainly isn't thin, but it is delicious !

Here is a beautiful egg sweet, also suitable as an invalid dish :—

ZABAGLIONE

1 egg yolk per person, plus 1 extra for every 3 yolks. 1 teaspoon sugar per person. 1 measure marsala. 1 pinch of salt.

For hot zabaglione :—Place all ingredients in a clean basin and whip together. Place basin over hot (NOT BOILING) water, and continue to whisk steadily until a stiff consistency is obtained. Remove from water, continue to whisk, then pour into glasses. Serve right away with sponge fingers. The secret of a successful zabaglione is that it must be brought to boiling point but must NOT BOIL or it will curdle.

For cold zabaglione :—As above, but carry on mixing over ice until consistency becomes quite cold, then add half the quantity of whipped cream. Prepare in each glass a small square of sponge soaked in marsala, pour in the mixture and serve very cold.

Note.—Rum, brandy, sherry or whisky may be used instead of marsala.

Recipes which may be served as hors d'œuvres, savoury, or as an informal snack with iced lager, beer or hot coffee.

PIZZA (serves 6)

2 lb. flour. 1 cup warm water. 1 oz. yeast. 1 medium-sized tin peeled tomatoes, chopped. 1 clove of garlic, chopped. 1 teaspoon mixed herbs. Pinch of salt. Anchovy fillets.

Dissolve yeast in warm water; add yeast and water to flour. Knead the dough thoroughly until the dough is firm. Cover dough with clean cloth; let it rise. Meanwhile, add chopped garlic, anchovies, mixed herbs and salt to tomatoes, making a thick sauce. Cut dough into equal pieces and roll out each piece and shape into 6 large rounds. Spread each round with the sauce and fry in an inch of smoking hot oil or fat until golden brown both sides. Pierce with a fork; if fork comes out clean, pizza is well cooked!

QUICHE LORRAINE

Short pastry (puff or flaky pastry also suitable). 5 rashers of bacon. Fine slices of Gruyère cheese. 2 eggs. ½ oz. flour. ¼ pint fresh milk. Seasoning of salt, cayenne pepper and pinch of nutmeg. ¼ oz. butter, melted.

Line flan case with pastry. Place on the bottom *lightly grilled* rashers of bacon, cover with fine slices of cheese. Beat eggs into flour, add milk, seasoning and melted butter; strain into case. Bake for 20 to 30 minutes or until set and lightly browned. Serve sliced into portions, hot or cold.

A favourite savoury or informal snack :—

WELSH RAREBIT

Rough-grate 4 *oz. Cheddar cheese.* ¼ *pint of ale.* 1 *pinch English mustard.* 4 *pieces of toast. Dash Worcester sauce. Seasoning of salt, pepper and cayenne pepper.*

Boil ale, add mustard and Worcester sauce. Reduce the beer to half the quantity and stir in the cheese. Take off the fire and stir until it is smooth. Season. Pour over hot buttered toast, brown under the grill, and serve piping hot.

Note.—This is on old English recipe dating from 1742.

VEGETABLES,
SALADS AND FRUIT

*When purchasing it is worth
while bearing in mind the
economy and fresh vitamin
value of seasonal produce.
Why not treat vegetables the
French way and introduce them
as a complete course after the
meat dish!
Braised endive, celery, lettuce,
stuffed eggplants, artichoke
hearts are all ideal as a
vegetable course.*

VEGETABLES

TO BOIL ROOT VEGETABLES

After thoroughly cleaning in cold water, cut out all bruised or dark places, scrub or peel, and start cooking in enough cold water to barely cover them, add salt to taste. When boiling, lower the heat and cover tightly. There should be no water to drain off when vegetables are done.

TO BOIL GREEN VEGETABLES

After thoroughly cleaning in cold water, cut out all bruised or dark places, bring water in pot to the boil, add salt to taste, then place vegetables in. Re-boil as quickly as possible ; the cooking must be fast to retain the green colour. Do NOT leave green vegetables in the cooking water for any length of time. When tender, drain and serve at once. In the case of peas and beans, these may be cooked and re-heated when required. The water that is so often thrown away from cooking green vegetables has as much of the flavour and goodness of the vegetables in it as the soup stock has of the meat and it can be used for soups, gravies, stews, etc.

TO BOIL DRIED VEGETABLES

Soak overnight in cold water ; put in *un*salted boiling water and boil for $1\frac{1}{2}$ to 2 hours ; drain, season and serve at once.

ARTICHOKES VINAIGRETTE

1 *artichoke per person.*

Break off stem close to leaves, remove outside leaves, cut off 1 inch from top. Tie with string to keep shape. Soak in cold water ; drain ; cook in boiling salted water for 30 minutes to 1 hour, according to size. Drain well ; remove string ; cut out choke (the thistle-like filling in the centre of the artichoke). Serve with vinaigrette or lemon and oil dressing.

ARTICHOKE HEARTS

Boil in the usual manner, then remove the leaves, and eat the hearts—either cold with vinaigrette dressing or hot with melted butter and a little grated Parmesan cheese.

ASPARAGUS MILANAISE

Allow 12 asparagus per person. 2 cups grated Parmesan cheese. 2 oz. butter. 4 eggs.

Carefully scrape lower part of each asparagus stalk ; wash well and tie into bundles of 12. Cook in boiling salted water, standing upright, for 20 to 30 minutes. Place on a dish, remove all water, sprinkle heads liberally with Parmesan cheese, cover with nut-brown butter—butter should froth on contact with the dish—and place a fried egg on top of each portion before serving. Serve very hot.

ASPARAGUS WITH MELTED BUTTER

Allow 12 asparagus per person. 2 oz. butter.

Carefully scrape lower part of each asparagus stalk ; wash well and tie into bundles of 12. Cook, standing upright, in boiling salted water for 20 to 30 minutes. Drain. Serve hot, with melted butter apart.

Asparagus make a fine soup : —

ASPARAGUS SOUP

24 heads of asparagus. 1½ pints vegetable stock or water. 1 oz. flour. 1 oz. butter or margarine. Seasoning of salt and pepper. Bay-leaf. Sprigs of parsley. 1 oz. lean bacon, diced. 1 cup cream. 1 egg yolk.

Wash asparagus and carefully scrape stalks ; cut off points and retain ; slice remainder of stalks into 1½ inch dice. Melt butter in a large sauce-pan, add asparagus and bacon ; add bay-leaf and parsley. Add stock, season, and let simmer slowly for 1½ hours. When ready, pass through a sieve. Re-heat, then remove from fire and add flour ; stir in slowly cream and egg yolk beaten together well. Place over low fire and thicken the mix-ture, continually stirring. BUT DO NOT BOIL. Add points of asparagus (cooked). Serve with croûtons, and pass round separately grated Par-mesan cheese.

AUBERGINE FRIED

1 *eggplant per person. Seasoning of salt and pepper.*

Peel and thinly slice eggplants, dust with flour. Place in a light frying batter and fry in deep fat until golden-brown, drain well, season. Serve very hot.

AUBERGINE STUFFED

Mark outer shell with a knife, slice in 2 length-wise. DO NOT PEEL. Deep-fry for 5 minutes, scoop out the centres, mix well together with equal quantity of peeled and chopped tomatoes and field mushroom stalks ; season, replace in the skins, sprinkle with grated cheese and brown in the oven or under the grill.

BROAD BEANS AU BEURRE

2 *lb. broad beans.* 1 *oz. butter. Seasoning of pep-per.*

It is important when purchasing broad beans in the pod that the ones selected should be small, young, tender, with velvety outsides. Feel the outsides with the fingers ; they should be soft and juicy. Reject the large dry discoloured pods.

Shell the beans and cook at once in salted boiling water. When tender, drain well. Return them to saucepan, season, add a few dabs of butter, and toss lightly until butter is melted in with the beans. Serve at once.

BRUSSELS SPROUTS

1 *quart Brussels sprouts. Dabs of butter.*

Cook in fast-boiling salted water. Drain well. Serve with a dab of butter.

BRUSSELS SPROUTS RISSOLÉS

1 *quart Brussels sprouts, select small fresh green ones.*

Boil. Drain well. Sauté in a frying-pan, jerking occasionally to prevent the sprouts sticking to the pan. Serve dry and hot.

CABBAGE

Take off outside leaves, cut in quarters, remove tough stalks. Shred or not, as desired. Wash well, boil in salted water, drain, season with butter, salt and pepper.

CARROTS VICHY

2 *lb. young carrots, finely sliced.* ½ *oz. butter or margarine. Seasoning of salt and pepper.* 1 *teaspoon sugar.* ⅛ *pint water.*

Place carrots in saucepan, add butter, sugar water, season and cover tightly. Simmer until cooked. Remove lid and leave on fire until liquor has completely reduced. Carrots will have a delicious flavour and a fine brilliance.

CAULIFLOWER POLONAISE

1 *large cauliflower*. 1 *hard-boiled egg, chopped*.
Seasoning of salt and pepper. Chopped parsley.
½ *cup bread-crumbs.*

Cut off coarse stalk of cauliflower and remove
part of thick stem ; soak in cold salted water,
wash well, rinse. Boil, cool, drain, season, and
shallow-fry until brown. Place on a dish. Put a
little butter in a pan, heat, add bread-crumbs,
fry until brown ; add egg and parsley, then pour
over the cauliflower. Serve very hot.

CHESTNUT PURÉE

24 *chestnuts, peeled. Milk*. 2 *oz. butter. Seasoning of salt, pepper and* 1 *teaspoon sugar.*

Cook chestnuts in milk until very soft ; drain, and
pass through a sieve or mash with fork. Place
in a saucepan, add a little of the milk. Re-boil.
Season, and mix in butter. Serve very hot.

ENDIVE FLAMANDE

8 *pieces of Belgian endive.* 1 *oz. butter or margarine.* ½ *lemon. Seasoning of salt and pepper.*

Wash the endives. Place in a pan. Add lemon
juice and butter or margarine, season, cover with
greaseproof paper. Cook in oven until tender.
(No liquid is required.) Remove. Reduce stock
and pour over the endives.
Superb with a slice of beef marrow-bone on top !

*Note.—Braised Belgian endive or braised celery
or braised lettuce, cooked slowly, tightly covered,
with a dash of water, lemon juice, seasoning,
makes a nice change served with the roast.*

FRENCH BEANS (Haricots verts)

2 lb. French or string beans. Seasoning of salt and pepper.

Select beans that are velvety to the touch and moist inside. Remove the ends ; in a perfect bean there should be no strings. Boil. Drain, season, and serve with a knob of butter.

LENTILS

2 cups dried lentils. 3 cloves. 1 tablespoon butter. 1 carrot. 1 bouquet garni. Pepper. 1 onion. ½ teaspoon salt.

Soak lentils overnight in cold water to cover. Drain. Place in cold water, bring to the boil ; add carrot, onion stuck with cloves, bouquet garni ; when nearly cooked, add salt ; finish cooking. Drain. Remove seasonings. Add butter and pepper. Serve very hot.

MARROW

Peel marrow and cut into 4 lengthwise ; trim into even pieces, and remove seeds. Put in a steamer, season with salt and steam for 20 to 30 minutes. Strain. Serve with white sauce and garnish with chopped parsley.

MARROWS PROVENÇALE

4 baby marrows, finely sliced. 1 clove of garlic, peeled and chopped. 2 tomatoes, peeled and chopped. Seasoning of salt and pepper. 1 onion, finely sliced.

Place a little margarine or butter in a saucepan, heat, add marrows and shallow-fry for 5 minutes ; add onion, garlic and tomatoes ; season ; cover and cook slowly for 30 minutes.

REMNANTS

PEAS À LA FRANÇAISE

1 pint shelled peas. 1 lettuce. Seasoning of salt and pepper. 12 button onions. 1 teaspoon sugar. 1 oz. butter.

Wash and finely shred lettuce. Mix the butter, peas, lettuce and onions together, barely cover with water, season, and add sugar. Cover and simmer until tender.

PEAS À LA MENTHE

1 lb. shelled peas (small as possible). ½ teaspoon sugar. 1 oz. butter. Sprig of mint.

Boil peas. Add sugar and mint. Finish boiling gently. Strain, and serve with mint and a dab of butter.

PEAS PAYSANNE

1 tin peas (small as possible). 6 small onions. Pinch of sugar. 1 carrot, sliced. Seasoning of salt, pepper and chopped lettuce leaf.

Place carrot in a pan with onions, add stock from the peas, and simmer slowly until tender. Add peas, seasoning and pinch of sugar. Drain before serving.

POINTS OF ASPARAGUS

Snap each asparagus stalk approximately halfway and make the tops into little bundles. Place, standing upright, in boiling salted water and cook until tender. Drain. Serve very hot with a dab of butter on top of each portion.

PURÉE OF PEAS

Boil green peas until tender, drain, pass through a sieve, season with salt, pepper and butter.

PURPLE BROCCOLI AU PARMESAN

4 purple broccoli. ½ cup grated Parmesan cheese.

Trim but leave a little leaf. Clean and boil. Sprinkle with grated Parmesan cheese. Cook a little butter until frothy, and pour over broccoli before serving.

RED CABBAGE

¼ bottle red wine. 1 red cabbage, finely shred. Bacon rind. Seasoning of salt, pepper and finely chopped apple. 1 onion. 1 carrot. ¼ pint stock. 4 cloves.

Wash well the red cabbage, place into a saucepan, add onion stuck with cloves, carrot, a little bacon rind, wine, seasoning and stock. Cover and braise slowly for 2½ hours.

SPINACH FLORENTINE

4 lb. spinach. 2 cloves of garlic. 4 fillets of anchovies, cut into tiny pieces. Seasoning of salt and pepper.

Remove all the stalks from the spinach, wash well in plenty of water 2 or 3 times. Cook in fast-boiling salted water until tender. Remove. Drain well and squeeze to remove all the water. Season. Heat a little oil in a frying-pan, add garlic, cook for 2 or 3 minutes. Discard garlic. Add spinach, shake with a fork. Add anchovies to the spinach. Mix well. Serve very hot.

SPINACH

Remove all stalks from spinach, wash well in plenty of water 2 or 3 times. Cook in fast-boiling salted water until tender. Remove. Drain well and chop finely or pass through a sieve, and re-heat. Serve with a knob of butter.

227

Potatoes are so popular and may be cooked in so many ways, that it is worth devoting a little more space to some of these recipes.

NEW POTATOES

Boil in their skins; peel when cooked. Decorate with mint leaves.

NEW POTATOES PERSILLÉS

1½ lb. small new potatoes, boiled. Melted butter. Parsley, finely chopped.

Pour butter over potatoes, then roll them in parsley.

MASHED POTATOES

4 lb. potatoes. 1 oz. butter or margarine. ¼ pint milk. Grated nutmeg. Seasoning of salt and pepper.

Boil potatoes, drain, replace on the fire to exude all water. Mash quickly. Add boiling milk and butter. Stir briskly with a wooden spoon, season, and add a little grated nutmeg.

BYRON POTATOES

4 large potatoes, cooked in their jackets. Seasoning of salt and pepper.

Remove the potato with a spoon, crush lightly with a fork, add seasoning. Place in a hot pan. press down evenly with a fork, cook in the oven until brown. Remove, place on a dish, cover with a little cream; sprinkle with grated Parmesan cheese, and brown under the grill.

POTATOES À LA CRÈME

1 *lb. new potatoes. Seasoning of salt and pepper.*
1 *cup milk.*

Peel and slice potatoes, cook in milk, season. Simmer slowly until tender.

POTATOES ALLUMETTES

2 *cups potatoes, cut into match-like strips. Seasoning of salt and pepper.*

Fry in deep fat and season to taste.

POTATOES AMANDINE

2 *oz. almonds or any dried nuts. 2 lb. potatoes.*
1 *egg yolk. Seasoning of salt, pepper, nutmeg.*

Boil potatoes, drain and dry-mash. Replace over stove and work in egg yolk. Cook on full fire for 2 minutes, stirring continually. Add seasoning. Divide the mixture into small pieces, roll into balls. Pass through a little milk and crumb with crushed nuts. Fry in deep fat. Drain. Dust with salt.

POTATOES ANNA

4 *lb. potatoes, peeled. Seasoning of salt and pepper.*
2 *oz. fat or oil.*

Slice the potatoes as thinly as possible in shapes the size of a penny, season. Prepare a flat sauté-pan by placing in the oil and allowing to become red-hot. Dry the potatoes in a cloth, arrange in design at bottom of the pan and around the sides. Cook in the oven, pressing them down from time to time. Ready when golden-brown. Turn out and cut into portions.

POTATOES AU FOUR

1 *large potato per person.*

Scrub well, place on a bed of rock salt. Bake in the oven. When cooked, cut 2 crossed gashes across each ; pinch potato gently at base so that it opens out and, in opening, put a dab of butter and a pinch of salt. Serve each one on a separate plate.

POTATOES AU GRATIN

Arrange mashed potatoes in a dish, sprinkle with grated Parmesan cheese, and brown in the oven.

POTATOES MACAIRE

4 *large potatoes. Seasoning of salt and pepper.*

Bake potatoes in their jackets. When ready, scoop the potatoes from their jackets, season and crush. Spread in a greased pan about $1\frac{1}{2}$ inches deep with a dab of butter on top. Bake in the oven. When golden-brown, turn over completely and bake the other side. Ready when a golden-brown colour.

POTATOES PARISIENNE

With a potato cutter, scoop out little round balls of potatoes ; fry in a little butter until brown, season, and finish in the oven.

POTATOES PARMENTIER

Cut potatoes in $\frac{1}{2}$ inch dice, shallow-fry until brown, season, finish in the oven.

POTATOES SAUTÉ

Slice potatoes and shallow-fry until brown, season, sprinkle with chopped parsley.

With vegetable remnants make : —

RATATOUILLE (a vegetable stew)

(There are many variations regarding this particular recipe but the real interpretation, from my point of view, is this one used by French housewives generally to transform all vegetable left-overs into a very good dish.)
Fry sliced onion in equal proportions of oil and butter, together with crushed cloves of garlic, until brown. Then add whatever left-over vegetables at your disposal—marrows, aubergines, French beans, peas, etc. Fry all together for 4 minutes ; add fresh tomatoes peeled and crushed or 1 tablespoon tomato purée. Cover and cook in the oven for about 20 minutes.
May be served as a tasty garnish but, if desired, may be served as a main dish with added eggs scrambled into the vegetable mixture and served immediately.

Cooked vegetables may be used also for : —

CREAM VEGETABLE SOUP

1 *lb. mixed cooked vegetables.* 1 *cup vegetable stock.* 1 *cup white sauce. Seasoning of salt and pepper.*

Boil all the ingredients for 3 minutes ; strain through sieve and season to taste. Pass round separately grated Parmesan cheese.

SALADS

AUGUSTIN SALAD

French beans, lettuce, quartered tomatoes, hard-boiled egg, served with mayonnaise dressing with dash of Worcester sauce.

COS LETTUCE ROMAINE À L'ESTRAGON

Wash well cos lettuce; cut in 4 lengthwise; sprinkle with chopped tarragon. Serve with desired dressing.

CHIFFONADE SALAD

Celery cut into match-shaped strips, lettuce, chicory, endives, tomatoes, beetroot, hard-boiled eggs quartered, and serve with vinaigrette dressing.

CURLY ENDIVE SALAD (perfect game salad)

Curly endive with vinaigrette dressing.

ENDIVE SALAD

Wash well 4 pieces of Belgian endive, drain off all the water, cut into suitable pieces, place in salad-bowl. Add salad dressing just before serving.

ENDIVE AND CAPSICUM SALAD (excellent with game)

Endive and sliced red peppers mixed together well; serve with vinaigrette or lemon dressing.

FOUR SEASONS SALAD

Lettuce, beetroot or tomato, cooked potatoes, cooked peas, arranged in 4 quarters on a dish; pour mayonnaise dressing over potatoes, vinegar over tomatoes, oil over lettuce.

ITALIAN SALAD

Mixed vegetables with fillets of anchovies and dice of salami, served with mayonnaise dressing.

JAPANESE SALAD

Mix the leaves of a lettuce, a few slices of banana and orange, a few seeded grapes, pineapple and walnut, and serve with Japanese mayonnaise dressing.

LETTUCE SALAD À LA CIBOULETTE

Wash well a lettuce, drain, and sprinkle with chopped chives. Serve with vinaigrette dressing.

LORETTE SALAD (a very good poultry salad)

Mix together well 1 lb. corn salad (mâche), 1 beetroot cut into fine strips, 3 sticks celery cut into fine strips. Serve with vinaigrette dressing.

ORANGE AND LETTUCE SALAD (with game, duck, etc.)

Sections of oranges, free from all white pith, dressed with hearts of lettuces, and served with vinaigrette dressing.

ORANGE SALAD (with game, duck, etc.)

Remove pith from 8 orange quarters with a sharp knife. (Remove flesh only.) Serve very cold, sprinkle with a few drops of kirsch; or, if preferred, vinaigrette dressing.

POINTS OF ASPARAGUS SALAD

Snap each asparagus stalk approximately halfway and make the tops into little bundles. Place, standing upright, in boiling salted water and cook until tender. Cool. Drain. Serve with vinaigrette dressing.

POTATO SALAD

Pour mayonnaise dressing over boiled diced potatoes and sprinkle with chopped parsley.

RUSSIAN SALAD (as an accompaniment or as a cold filling)

Carrots and turnips and potatoes cleaned and cut into small "buttons," cooked and mixed with fresh cooked peas. The whole bound with mayonnaise dressing.

Note.—Left-over cooked carrots, turnips, potatoes and peas may be used.

TOMATO SALAD

Peel tomatoes by first warming them on fork over low heat or by dipping in boiling water for 10 seconds, cut into fine slices across the stalk. Serve with vinaigrette or mayonnaise dressing and sprinkle with chopped parsley.

WATERCRESS SALAD (delicious and the right item to include in a slimming diet !)

Watercress lavishly sprinkled with chopped parsley and serve with lemon and oil dressing.

WEBBS WONDER SALAD (serve with meats, poultry, etc.)

This is a particularly tender salad and is a cross between chicory and lettuce. Wash well, drain, sprinkle with chopped chives, and dress with vinaigrette dressing.

It is a matter of taste as to whether you wish to add, say, avocado pear, radishes, chives, spring onions, speck of garlic, or add fruits to certain salads; just as salad dressings may be varied according to taste (see Salad Dressings, pages 235-7).

SALAD DRESSINGS

Vinaigrette or French dressing blends with green salads which customarily accompany roasts, fries, grills, etc. It is also served with asparagus, artichokes, avocado pears, and various hors d'œuvres.

As oil separates quite easily from vinegar, MIX or SHAKE WELL with a small amount but, when a large amount required, it is preferable to mix in an electric mixer, if available.

Use the best olive oil, ensuring it is not rancid, and wine vinegar is preferable for malt vinegar kills the taste of any drinking wine. But lemon juice may replace vinegar.

VINAIGRETTE or FRENCH DRESSING

Dash of Worcester sauce. Dash of tabasco, if available. A little English and French mustard. Pepper and salt to taste.

Dilute the whole with vinegar and stir well; add oil at a 50-50 proportion, unless otherwise desired. Mix well, pour over the salad and mix before serving.

Variations of vinaigrette dressing: —

CALIFORNIAN DRESSING

Use grapefruit juice instead of vinegar.

PORTO RICO DRESSING

Use half vinegar and half lemon juice and add 2 tablespoons chopped olives and 1 tablespoon tomato ketchup.

MINT DRESSING

Add 2 tablespoons finely chopped fresh mint leaves.

INDIAN DRESSING

Add 2 finely chopped hard-boiled eggs, 1 tablespoon finely chopped red pepper, 1 tablespoon finely chopped green pepper, 1 tablespoon finely chopped parsley, mix well, chill and shake before serving.

CREAM DRESSING (this is a delightful lettuce salad dressing)

Replace oil with cream.

CHIFFONADE DRESSING

Add 2 finely chopped hard-boiled eggs, 1 tablespoon grated onion, 2 tablespoons finely chopped pickled beets, 1 teaspoon finely chopped green olives, 1 tablespoon finely chopped chervil or parsley.

CHUTNEY DRESSING

Use half vinegar and half lemon, add $\frac{1}{2}$ cup finely chopped chutney.

RUSSIAN DRESSING

Add 2 tablespoons chili sauce, 2 tablespoons finely chopped red or green pepper and $\frac{1}{2}$ teaspoon onion juice.

Mayonnaise dressing blends with a variety of vegetable and fruit salads which customarily accompany a cold course.
To redress a mayonnaise that has curdled, try putting 1 tablespoon boiling water in another basin and whisk continually whilst gradually dropping the sauce into the water ; or, beat additional egg yolks separately then beat in the curdled mixture slowly.

MAYONNAISE DRESSING

1 *egg yolk*. 1 *teaspoon vinegar*. $\frac{1}{8}$ *pint olive oil*. 3 *dashes lemon juice. Seasoning of salt, pepper and pinch of mustard.*

Beat together in a basin the yolk, lemon juice, vinegar and seasoning. Add oil slowly, beating continually until a stiff consistency is obtained.

Variations of mayonnaise dressing:—

CHUTNEY DRESSING

Add 2 tablespoons chutney and mix well.

CREAM MAYONNAISE

Add 2 tablespoons whipped cream ; also, paprika and fruit juices may be added.

JAPANESE MAYONNAISE

Add 2 tablespoons cream to 1 tablespoon mayonnaise, juice of $\frac{1}{2}$ orange, seasoning of salt and pepper.

GREEN MAYONNAISE

Colour green by adding spinach juice or vegetable colouring.

RED MAYONNAISE

Add 1 tablespoon tomato ketchup, tomato purée, tomato juice, vegetable colouring or sieved lobster coral.

RUSSIAN DRESSING

Add 1 tablespoon drained chili sauce, 1 tablespoon diced pimento, 1 tablespoon diced green pepper, 1 tablespoon diced celery.

THOUSAND ISLAND DRESSING

Add $\frac{1}{4}$ cup whipped cream to Russian dressing.

HOT MAYONNAISE

2 *egg yolks. 2 tablespoons olive oil. 1 tablespoon vinegar. 2 tablespoons hot water. Seasoning of salt and cayenne pepper. Chopped parsley.*

Gradually add oil to egg yolks, pour on slowly vinegar and water ; continually stirring, cook in a bain-marie until a stiff consistency is obtained ; season and sprinkle with parsley.

FRUIT

STEWED FRUIT

Using fresh fruit. Prepare by washing or wiping, peel and cut, as desired. Put in a pan, barely cover with water, add sugar (1 cup sugar to 1 lb. fruit), and juice of 1 lemon. Cover and stew over gentle heat. When ready, remove fruit to a dish. Boil syrup until thick and pour over the fruit.

Using dried fruit. Wash and soak in cold water for several hours. Put in a pan, barely cover with water, add sugar to taste. Stew gently until tender. When ready, remove fruit to a dish. Boil syrup until thick and pour over the fruit.

JAM (this is a simple recipe)

Fruits (should be ripe, sound, dry, clean)   *ater.*

Apple (peeled)	1 *gill to 1 lb.*
Blackberry and apple	*Barely cover.*
Blackcurrant	1 *gill to 1 lb.*
Damson	*Barely cover.*
Gooseberry	1 *gill to 1 lb.*
Plum	*Barely cover.*
Redcurrant	,, ,,
Rhubarb	,, ,,
Strawberry	,, ,,
Vegetable marrow	,, ,,

Use equal weight of sugar as fruit.

Cook fruit with water until tender, regularly breaking it with a wooden spoon. Add heated sugar and boil rapidly, skimming if necessary, for 10 to 20 minutes, stirring continually. (Put a little jam on a cold plate and run a finger lightly over the top; if jam is sufficiently cooked, a wrinkled skin will show.) Bottle the jam while still warm, NOT HOT. Tie down firmly with damp greaseproof paper or jam cover, and store in a dark cool place.

Note.—Jam should be cooked in a copper, aluminium or enamel lined pan.

SOFT FRUITS

With regard to soft fruits, a little care in buying is worth while. Lightly toss the fruit in the basket to ensure that underneath a few choice specimens there is not a sodden mass. Particularly in the case of raspberries, see that the basket is dry; red-stained baskets should be treated with suspicion.

Also, soft fruits are inclined to shrink during the cooking process of bottling.

BOTTLING FRUIT

Use clean and dry glass bottling jars. Wipe or wash fruit and pack closely in the jars; place jars in a lukewarm oven until fruit skin is cracking; then fill jars to the top with BOILING water. Immediately place on rubber ring and glass lid; firmly screw metal "collar", then loosen half a turn (or put on ring, cap and clip, according to type used.) Allow to get cold before storing in a cool dark place.

FRUIT SALAD

¼ *pint water. 1 oz. sugar. 2 bananas, peeled and sliced. 2 apples, peeled and sliced. 4 apricots, stoned and sliced. 4 plums, finely sliced and stoned. 1 fresh peach, skinned and sliced. 2 pears, peeled and sliced. Grapes, halved and seeded. ½ lb. cherries, stoned. Redcurrants.*

Put water and sugar in a saucepan, boil for 10 minutes. Remove. Allow to cool, then pour into a serving-bowl and add all the fruits. Add 1 measure of kirsh, maraschino or any liqueur desired.

Note.—Varieties of fruits may be changed or added, according to taste. Also, fruit salad may be made with many left-over cooked fruits.

Recipes which may be served as a first course: —

AVOCADO PEAR

½ *avocado pear per person.*

Great care should be exercised in the selection of the pears. An avocado pear should be soft all over and evenly green, one hard spot and it is no good. Cut pear in half, remove the large stone. Fill each portion with well-mixed vinaigrette dressing, and serve with small spoon.

GRAPEFRUIT

½ *grapefruit per person.*

Prepare grapefruit well in advance. Cut in half crosswise; cut around each segment so that it can be removed easily. Sprinkle generously with sugar and place a maraschino cherry in the centre of each half. Keep in a cold place until ready to serve. Serve with small spoon.

HONEYDEW MELON (in season in winter)

1 *slice of honeydew melon per person.*

Cut in narrow sections. Serve very cold with sugar and ground ginger.

MELON (other varieties)

1 slice of melon per person.

Remove seeds and stringy portion. Serve very cold with castor sugar and ground ginger.

FIGS AND SMOKED HAM

Arrange very thin slices of smoked ham or *coppa* on a dish with figs in the centre. (Allow 3 peeled figs per portion. Figs are in season in the autumn). Serve cold.

And don't forget about the delicious pineapple which makes a superb sweet dessert: ~

A pineapple should be an even sunny-gold colour. If the stem is rather loose, it is beginning to get over-ripe ; if it has too many dark spots on the surface, it is frozen. Cut off top and base ; peel across, and remove core. (Skin may be simmered with water and sugar to obtain pineapple syrup).

PINEAPPLE AU KIRSCH

1 slice pineapple per person (tinned pineapple slice suitable). 1 measure of kirsch (any desired liqueur, brandy or rum, may be used instead, and this is where the purchase of a miniature bottle comes in handy!). Sprinkling of castor sugar

Pour kirsch over pineapple and sprinkle well with sugar. (Best to prepare all portions in the one dish and allow to macerate awhile, if possible, in the refrigerator.) Serve very cold.

Many fruits, such as raspberries, quartered peaches and orange segments, strawberries, etc., may be served in the same way.

PINEAPPLE FLAMBÉE

1 or 2 slices pineapple per person. Lemon and orange rind. 1 measure of kirsch. 1 tablespoon water. 1 tablespoon sugar.

Place pineapple slices in tureen, add a little rind of lemon and orange, water, sugar, cover and cook for approximately 10 minutes. Add kirsch and set alight. Serve at once.

Peeled bananas, nectarines, skinned peaches, may be used in the same way. By the way, to test ripeness of a fresh peach, apply slight pressure with thumb and forefinger; it should "give" and feel soft.

VARIOUS CHEESES

Serve cheeses as a dessert with unsalted crackers or French bread. Two varieties should be offered to guests—one soft, one hard. Ensure a cheese is in a ripe and proper condition when purchasing it. Do not overcook cheese mixtures such as rarebits and sauces.

BEL PAESE (Italian). Soft cheese, rich and mild.

BRIE (French). Soft cheese, Camembert-type, made in thin circles and has rich delicate flavour. Ripe when creamy, almost running.

CAERPHILLY (Welsh). National Welsh cheese, hard, whole-milk, crumbly and tangy.

CAMEMBERT (French). Soft cheese, sold in flat round boxes, is creamy and the soft rind may be eaten too ; should be eaten when top is soft to touch, then inside will be runny ; will not keep long once box is opened.

CARRÉ DE L'EST (French). Soft cheese.

CHEDDAR (English). Hard cheese, mellow ; keeps well if dried thoroughly and placed in air-tight jars, and is good cooking cheese.

CHESHIRE (English) England's oldest cheese, hard. Crumbly in texture, creamy without being soft, and has sharp flavour ; delicious with crusty fresh bread and butter. Keeps well. (Red—mild ; Blue and White—stronger.)

CREAM (English). Made from sour milk curds ; used a lot in salads, and especially good with fruit.

DEMI-SEL (Swiss). Cream cheese, milder than English cream cheese.

DUNLOP (Scottish). Hard cheese, similar to Cheddar.

EDAM & GOUDA (Dutch). Hard cheeses. Round shape with red or golden rinds ; mild and unsuitable cooking cheeses.

FROMAGE DE MONSIEUR (French). Soft cheese.

GLOUCESTER (English). Hard cheese. Single Gloucester—a spring white cheese ; Double Gloucester, Red or Yellow— similar to Cheddar and fine flavoured.

GRUYÈRE	(Swiss). Hard cheese ; mild, sweet, with many holes, and excellent cooking cheese.
LANCASHIRE	(English). Hard cheese, similar to Cheshire ; well known in its country as a toasting cheese.
LEICESTER	(English). Hard cheese, similar to Cheddar ; keeps well.
LIMBURGER	(Belgian). Soft cheese, whole-milk, strong smelling and full in flavour.
MAROILLES	(French). Soft cheese.
NEUFCHÂTEL	(French). Cream cheese, rich and spicy.
NOKKELOST	(Swedish). Loaf-shaped, spicy.
PARMESAN	(Italian). Very hard cheese, mature when about four years old ; excellent for grating and for cooking.
PASTORELLA	(Italian). Soft cheese.
PETIT-SUISSE	(Swiss). Cream cheese.
PONT-L'ÉVÊQUE	(French). Soft cheese, made in Normandy.
PORT SALUT	(French). Soft cheese, mild.
QUARTIROLO	(Italian). Soft cheese ; ripe when creamy, almost running.
SLIPCOTE	(English). Soft cheese, ripened between cabbage leaves.
WENSLEYDALE	(English). Tasty Yorkshire cheese. (Two varieties—a white cheese and another similar to Stilton.)

And here is a selection of blue cheeses :—

Blue cheese is creamy in colour with blue veining, has strong flavour and is unsuitable cooking cheese ; ripe when blue and creamy, when white and chalky it is tasteless.

BLUE DORSET (VINNEY)	(English). Blue cheese ; this *is* inclined to be hard and white, with horizontal veins.

CASTELLOE-BLANCO	(Portuguese). Blue cheese.
CABRALES	(Spanish). Blue cheese.
DANISH BLUE	(Danish). Blue cheese, similar to Roquefort.
DOLCE VERDE	(Italian). Blue cheese.
GORGONZOLA	(Northern Italian). Blue cheese, sharp flavoured, made and matured in the Italian mountains.
ROQUEFORT	(French). Blue cheese, rich and mellow, made from ewes' milk; used a lot in salads, and especially good with fruit.
STILTON	(English). Blue cheese; an aristocratic cheese which is fully mature at six months but better still at a year!
ZIN	(Swiss). Blue cheese.

APPENDIX

AVERAGE-TIME TABLE

FOR MEATS

Meat boned and rolled—25 minutes to lb., 25 minutes over. Chops (grill, fry)—10 to 20 minutes.

BEEF (roast)—16 minutes to lb. for rare beef, 16 to 22 minutes to lb. for medium beef, 30 minutes to lb. for well done beef.

BEEF (boil)—20 minutes to lb., 15 minutes over.

RUMP OR FILLET STEAK (grill, fry)—10 to 15 minutes, according to thickness and degree of cooking desired.

SALT BEEF (boil)—20 minutes to lb., 15 minutes over.

LAMB—Best end (roast)—20 to 30 minutes. Leg (roast)— $1\frac{1}{2}$ hours. Saddle (roast)—1 to $1\frac{1}{4}$ hours. Shoulder (roast)—1 hour.

MUTTON (boil)—20 minutes to lb., 15 minutes over. Best end (carré) (roast)—1 to $1\frac{1}{2}$ hours. Leg (roast)—$2\frac{1}{2}$ to 3 hours. Saddle (roast)—$2\frac{1}{2}$ hours. Shoulder (roast)—2 hours.

PORK (boil)—25 to 30 minutes to lb., 25 minutes over. Best end (roast)—$1\frac{1}{2}$ to 2 hours. Leg (roast)—2 to 3 hours. Loin (roast)—$1\frac{1}{2}$ to 2 hours. Sucking pig (roast)—$1\frac{3}{4}$ to 2 hours.

VEAL (boil)—25 minutes to lb., 25 minutes over. Best end (roast)—$1\frac{1}{2}$ to 2 hours. Leg (roast)—$3\frac{1}{2}$ to 4 hours. Stuffed shoulder (roast)—3 to $3\frac{1}{2}$ hours.

OX TONGUE (boil)—Large smoked—$4\frac{1}{2}$ hours. Small smoked— 3 hours. Large unsmoked—$3\frac{1}{2}$ hours. Small unsmoked—2 to $2\frac{1}{2}$ hours.

HAM AND BACON (boil)—$1\frac{1}{2}$ hours to 2 lb., $\frac{1}{2}$ hour each lb. over.

SAUSAGES (grill, fry). Pierce with fork before cooking—10 to 15 minutes.

KIDNEYS (grill, fry)—8 minutes approx.

LIVER (grill, fry)—4 to 6 minutes.

FOR POULTRY AND GAME

CAPON (roast)—1 to $1\frac{1}{2}$ hours.

CHICKEN (roast)—$\frac{1}{2}$ to 1 hours, according to size.

CHICKEN (boil) YOUNG—$\frac{3}{4}$ hours; BOILER $1\frac{1}{4}$ to $1\frac{1}{2}$ hours.

CHICKEN—Poussin or baby chicken (roast, grill)—15 to 20 minutes.

DUCK (roast)—1 hour, according to size.

DUCKLING (roast)—25 to 40 minutes, according to size.

DUCK, WILD (roast)—15 minutes (hot oven).

GOOSE (roast)—1 to 2 hours for 9 to 12 lb. $2\frac{1}{2}$ hours for 17 to 24 lb.

GROUSE (roast)—15 to 20 minutes (hot oven).

GUINEA FOWL (roast)—1 to $1\frac{1}{4}$ hours, according to size.

HARE (roast)—$1\frac{1}{2}$ to 2 hours.

PARTRIDGE (roast)—15 to 18 minutes (hot oven).

PHEASANT (roast)—30 to 40 minutes.

PLOVER (roast)—10 to 15 minutes (hot oven).

PIGEON, YOUNG (roast)—20 to 30 minutes.

PIGEON (stew)—1 to 2 hours approximately.

QUAIL (roast)—10 minutes (hot oven).

RABBIT (roast)—1 hour approximately.

SNIPE (roast)—8 to 10 minutes (hot oven).

TEAL (roast)—10 to 15 minutes (hot oven)

TURKEY (roast or bake)—$1\frac{1}{2}$ to 3 hours, according to size.

TURKEY (boil)—$1\frac{1}{2}$ to 2 hours, according to size.

VENISON (roast)—13 to 15 minutes to lb. and 15 minutes over.

WOODCOCK (roast)—12 to 15 minutes (very hot oven).

TABLE OF MEASURES (British Measure)

LIQUID MEASURES

3 teaspoons	1 tablespoon.
1 tablespoon	1 fluid oz.
3 tablespoons	$\frac{1}{8}$ pint or $\frac{1}{2}$ gill.
4 tablespoons	$\frac{1}{4}$ cup.
5 tablespoons	$\frac{1}{4}$ pint.
8 tablespoons	$\frac{1}{2}$ cup.
10 tablespoons	$\frac{1}{2}$ pint.
16 tablespoons	1 cup.
20 tablespoons	1 pint.
1 teacup	$\frac{1}{4}$ pint or 1 gill.
1 standard measuring cup or breakfastcup	$\frac{1}{2}$ pint.
2 cups	1 pint.
4 cups	2 pints or 1 quart.
1 measure or glass	1 wineglass.
4 fluid gills	1 pint.
2 pints	1 quart.
4 quarts	1 gallon.

Liquids	*Fluid or*	*Litres*
$\frac{1}{2}$ gill	$2\frac{1}{2}$ oz.	·7
1 gill.	5 oz.	·14
2 gills	10 oz.	·28
$\frac{1}{2}$ pint	10 oz.	·28
1 pint	20 oz.	·57
1 quart	40 oz.	1·14
1 gallon	160 oz.	4·54

DRY INGREDIENT MEASURES

Average Measure

1 teaspoon	$\frac{1}{4}$ oz.
1 dessertspoon	$\frac{1}{2}$ oz.
1 tablespoon	1 oz.
1 teacup	6 oz.

1 standard measuring cup
  or breakfastcup . . . . 8 oz. or ½ lb.

1 tablespoon butter or fat. . 1 oz.
½ cup butter or fat . . . . 4 oz. or ¼ lb.
1 cup butter or fat . . . . 8 oz. or ½ lb.
1 cup bread-crumbs, fresh   3 oz.
1 cup bread-crumbs, dry . 6 oz.
1 cup chopped meat . . . 8 oz. or ½ lb.
1 cup currants, sultanas, etc 6 oz.
1 cup flour . . . . 5 oz.
1 cup grated cheese . . . . 4 oz.
1 tablespoon honey, treacle,
  syrup . . . . 2 oz.
1 cup honey, treacle, syrup 14 oz.
½ cup mayonnaise . . . . . 4 oz.
1 cup rice . . . . 8 oz.
1 cup sugar, icing . . . 4½ oz.
1 cup sugar, granulated or
  castor . . . . 8 oz.
4 eggs with shells . . . . ½ lb.
5 eggs without shells . . . ½ lb.

*Note. — 1 tablespoon equals 2 dessertspoons or
4 teaspoons.*

*½ pint of liquid to the lb. is the average propor-
tion when mixing flour for dough, suet crust,
and scones.*

DRY MEASURE

4 gills . . . . 1 pint.
2 pints . . . . 1 quart.
2 quarts (4 pints) . . . . 1 pottle.
2 pottles (4 quarts) . . . 1 gallon.
2 gallons . . . . 1 peck.
4 pecks . . . . 1 bushel.
3 bushels . . . . 1 bag.
5 bushels (or porter's load) 1 sack of flour.

AVOIRDUPOIS WEIGHT

16 drachms . . . . 1 oz. (ounce).
16 oz. . . . . 1 lb. (pound).

28 lb.	1 qtr. (quarter).
4 qtrs.	1 cwt. (hundredweight).
20 cwts.	1 ton (ton).
8 stones	1 cwt. (hundredweight).
112 lb.	1 cwt. (hundredweight).

TABLE OF MEASURES (American Measures)

The "Hostess Dinner Book" brought me interesting correspondence from all over the world and, from American friends, many letters divulged a charming insistence that this next book should include a few comparative American and British weights and measures.
Here they are : —

The American Standard Cup measure is equivalent to the British Standard Cup, that is to say that they are both $\frac{1}{2}$ pint cups, but the liquid measure for the American cup is 8 fluid oz. and the British cup 10 fluid oz.

	American liquid measure	British liquid measure
$\frac{1}{2}$ pint	8 fluid oz. . .	10 fluid oz.
1 pint	16 fluid oz. . .	20 fluid oz.
2 tablespoons	1 fluid oz. . .	2 fluid oz.

DRY INGREDIENT MEASURES

	American cup	British cup
Butter, margarine, fat or lard .	8 oz.	8 oz.
Currants, sultanas, etc	5 oz.	6 oz.
Bread-crumbs, fresh	$1\frac{1}{2}$ oz.	3 oz.
Bread-crumbs, dry	$3\frac{1}{2}$ oz.	6 oz.
Flour	4 oz.	5 oz.
Grated cheese	4 oz.	4 oz.
Honey, treacle, syrup	11 oz.	14 oz.
Icing sugar	$4\frac{1}{2}$ oz.	$4\frac{1}{2}$ oz.
Sugar, granulated or castor . .	$7\frac{1}{2}$ oz.	8 oz.
Rice	8 oz.	8 oz.
Cornflour	6 oz.	6 oz.

SHOPPING OR SERVINGS CHART

(Basic Quantities to Allow)

Product	Quantity	For number of persons
SOUP	1 pint	3
FISH. SHELLFISH	1 or 2 fillets, or	1
	½ lb. fillets, fresh or frozen	1
	1 cutlet	1
	1 crab	3 or 4
	4 to 6 clams, or	1
	½ pint clams	4
	2 frogs' legs, or	1
	1 lb. frogs' legs	4
	1 lobster	3 or 4
	2 to 4 smelts, according to size	1
	6 scallops, or	1
	1 lb. scallops	1
	4 to 6 oysters, or	1
	½ pint oysters	4
	2 to 3 lb. whole fish	4
MEATS	*½ lb. per person when roasting as meat shrinks when roasted; 6 oz. per person when stewing as not such large shrinkage.*	
	3 cutlets	2
	3 meat croquettes	2
	3 meat patties	2
	1 large or 2 small veal, pork, lamb chops	1
	4 oz. sausages	1

VARIOUS MEATS AND OFFALS

	2 beef kidneys	4
	1 beef heart	4
	8 lamb kidneys	4
	1 lb. brains	4

Product	Quantity	For number of persons
	1 pair sweetbreads	4
	1½ lb. tripe	4
	4 lb. beef tongue	4
	4 to 6 oz. liver	1
	1 pig's trotter	1
POULTRY, GAME	1 chicken	4 to 6
	1 duck	4 to 6
	1 turkey	12 to 15
	1 hare	4 to 6
	1 rabbit	4 to 6
	1 partridge	1 to 2
	1 pheasant	2 to 4
VEGETABLES.	2½ lb. artichokes, or	6
	1 artichoke	1
	6 to 12 stalks asparagus . . .	1
	2½ lb. French or runner beans	6
	1 lb. beets	4
	1 peck broad beans	6
	1½ lb. broccoli	4
	1 lb. brussels sprouts	5
	1 large cabbage, or	6
	1 lb. cooked cabbage	4
	2 lb. carrots	6
	1 large cauliflower, or	6
	1½ lb. cauliflower	4
	½ lb. to 1 lb. celery	6
	1 lb. eggplant	4
	1 lb. small cooked onions . . .	4
	1 lb. parsnips	4
	2 lb. peas-in-pod	4
	1 lb. potatoes	4
	2 lb. spinach or greens	4
	1 lb. turnips	4

Product	*Quantity*	*For number of persons*
TEA	$\frac{1}{2}$ lb.	50
MILK	$\frac{1}{4}$ pint	1
MILK (for tea)	4 quarts	100
SUGAR	3 lb.	100
COFFEE (including milk)	$\frac{1}{2}$ pint	1

Note. — 1 tablespoon coffee to each 1 pint water.

1 pint milk to each 1 pint coffee.
1 lb. coffee to each 100 persons.
12 quarts milk for coffee for 100 persons.

BREAD	5 large loaves	100
BUTTER	$\frac{3}{4}$ lb. to each large loaf.	
CAKES	3 cakes or pieces of cake . .	1
PASTRY (for pies, etc.)		

$1\frac{1}{2}$ oz. to every 2 oz. sugar, flour,
etc. . . . . per head

POULTRY

CHICKEN OR DUCK

Place bird on side with leg at side of carver; with carving-knife cut through skin between leg and body, pull back leg with knife and disjoint from body; then cut off wing; remove leg and wing from other side in the same way; to remove breast, place bird on side and, by cutting the two joints at the front, the breast is gently and easily removed, cut into portions lengthwise; on each side of the backbone are two choice pieces of dark meat or "oysters" which are easily removable.

TURKEY Remove legs similarly, and serve each person with slices of breast and dark meat.

GOOSE Remove wish-bone or merry-thought by slipping knife through at the point of the breast, and proceed as above.

PHEASANT Breast rarely served whole, but sliced rather thick; drumsticks seldom served. (A small young pheasant may be split into two portions.)

GROUSE Rarely carved but served whole or split into two portions by cutting right through the centre from head to tail.

PARTRIDGE Served whole, or split in half.
PIGEON, PLOVER, SNIPE, TEAL DUCK OR WOODCOCK Usually served whole on toast.

FISH

SALMON

TURBOT, BRILL, AND FLAT-FISH GENERALLY

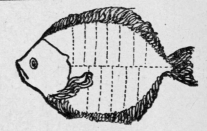